ODE TO COLOR

The Ten Essential Palettes for Living and Design

LORI WEITZNER

With Dorothy Mitchell

HARPER
DESIGN

An Imprint of HarperCollins Publishers

For Mike, Emma,
and Sophie

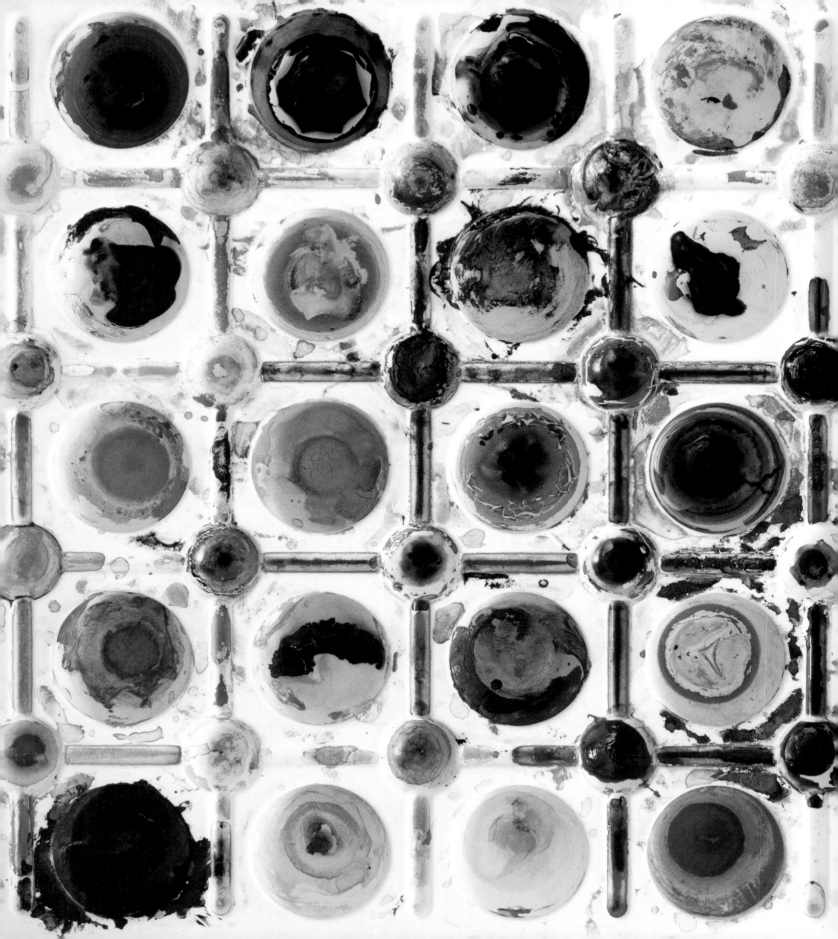

Contents

Introduction

As a girl, I drew and painted and created art mostly on my own, as the school system in the town where I grew up, about thirty miles outside New York City, did not have a very good art program. When I was eight, I started sketching fashion models wearing clothes that I designed for them, imagining that I would become a fashion designer one day. When I look back on those sketches now, I see that I paid a great deal of attention to the color and quality of the materials I used in my designs, to which I added much detail—trim, beads, fringe—and less attention to the structure and wearability of the clothing. Then, as now, I loved color and the various ways it played on different materials and in different light.

I was a junior in high school by the time my parents agreed to let me start art lessons. I knew by then that I wanted to study art in college, hopefully to make a career of painting, so two years later I enrolled at Syracuse University's School of Visual and Performing Arts. In my sophomore year, though, one of my professors matter-of-factly informed me that I would never make it as a painter. It was a crushing blow; it derailed my plans and aspirations and shook my confidence. But his observation that I was "good with composition and color" and should consider textile design (a field I had never heard of) was the seed from which my career—and passion—ultimately grew.

What I discovered in studying textiles was that color and color combinations in repeat patterns applied to fabrics—made to be worn or hung or sat upon—evoked stories, traditions, and places—and sometimes triggered memories and emotions. Textiles opened up the world of color to me in a way that painting never had. Where I saw the beach in one design, I could imagine ancient Egypt in another; a design might make me think of a Shakespeare play, visualize a shadowy film noir, or even conjure a memory about a long-forgotten place—its heat, its light, its smell. Textiles are alive and expressive, and I came to see them as more than a tapestry, more than a metaphorical summary of the threads of life experience, but as living things, weaving themselves into our lives and memories. I was smitten.

During college, I fell in love with the process of hand-painting silks. When I presented my senior thesis on this technique, my professor doubted that I would "go anywhere" in my career with them, but I didn't listen: with my portfolio of silks in hand, I landed my first job, in New York City, where I had always wanted to live and work.

My subsequent career path was a winding one that took me from designing for a bedding company to working as a freelance designer in Milan, then Zurich, and, finally, back in New York. By the time I completed this two-year loop, I had discovered that I needed the freedom that comes from working for myself, so I formed my own company and began selling my designs for a broad array of applications: fabrics and wallcoverings, dinnerware, stationery, rugs, and packaging for cosmetics companies. Eventually, my name was attached to those designs, and my brand was born.

Color is always at the foundation of my creations. It is the initial inspiration for all my designs and the guiding star throughout the design process. I have very particular notions of colors, their characters and impact and associations, both alone and in groups. Those notions have become templates from which I work; I refer to them as "color worlds," and they inform my aesthetic, consciously and subconsciously.

I have no set formula when it comes to developing a color world. For me it is not a science, but a process that is both intuitive and practical. Some of these worlds are the result of a deliberate attempt to conjure a certain mood, memory, place, or emotion. Others I have developed or discovered as I worked through color selections for my designs. In both instances, the process begins with an exploration of the contents of the thirty-six "color drawers" containing yarn and swatches of every color in the spectrum that I keep in my studio. For red alone, for example, I have six drawers, divided by their undertones, coolness, and warmth. I play with these materials, looking at them in varying intensities of light, mixing and matching them until I find what I am looking for—or it finds me.

I work in many color worlds, and know there are more to discover, but I've selected the ten featured in the chapters in this book because they are the most prominent in my work; they are the ones that have stood the test of time. They are personal to me, to my processes as an artist and to my life experiences. They are the primary threads in my tapestry—and I hope you'll find resonance in them too, as they correspond to the many gears we all move through in the course of our lives—work, reflection, rest, levity, and love. What connects them is a level of engagement: they speak to the senses on an emotional level, influencing our moods and jogging memory, and simply speaking to who we are, functioning as a form of self-expression.

This book—while it contains many interior design ideas and explores color from a cultural, religious, and social point of view—is foremost a journey through these distinct color worlds, each with its many powers, moods, and associations. I hope that in experiencing them, you'll be inspired to find your own.

1
Waterside

Now You See It

Water and sky: Blue is a primary color that pervades the natural world. It's the most popular color on the planet, and in the United States and Europe it is the favorite by an overwhelming margin. In a number of studies, roughly half of all people surveyed, both men and women alike, identify it as their preferred hue.

Blue is basic, accessible, and fundamental. But it is elusive, too, particularly in the natural world. A cup of seawater is not blue, but the ocean is, when the sun allows. The sky may be pure blue on a clear day, but you can't touch its color source or harvest it. The color blue was absent from Paleolithic cave paintings, because it is a color that cave dwellers couldn't extract from the earth itself.

Plants and minerals needed to make quality blue dyes and pigments were rare and expensive, relegating the color to a bit part in Western art until later in the Middle Ages, when trade routes allowed for lapis lazuli to be exported from Asia to the West. The Venetians called the mineral *ultramarinus* (meaning "beyond the sea"), and artists valued it for its beauty and rarity. During the Middle Ages, many artists used blue—it was the most expensive pigment of the day—to color the robes of the Virgin Mary, the most precious symbol of their faith. Blue became Mary's official color, securing its association with purity and sanctity, when Pope Pius V standardized the use of liturgical colors in the sixteenth century. In fashion, blue gained popularity as a color of nobility in the thirteenth century, when France's King Louis IX not only began wearing it but also gave it dominance in his family's coat of arms. The prestige that came to be associated with blue in the late Middle Ages survived over the ensuing centuries, making blue dyes and pigments valuable commodities.

The advent of synthetic blue pigments in the eighteenth century—science imitating life—loosened nature's grip on the color, and blue's prevalence and popularity soared. Blue is now an inexhaustible shape-shifter: it can be authoritative, confident, calm, cool, loyal, sad, intense, subdued, mysterious, or moody; it graces sanctuaries and clothes armies; it crosses art forms and cultural boundaries with remarkable power and ease. We see it, hear it, wear it, taste it, and feel it.

What's your blue?

Changeable
Prussian
Traditional
Familiar
Atlantic
Sky
Trustworthy
Navy
Indigo
Sapphire
Azure
Vast
Comfortable
Sea foam
Soothing
Enigmatic
Plaintive
Serene
Serious
Ink
Teal
Iceberg
Subdued
Aqua
Robin's egg
Contemplative
Blue spruce
Cobalt
Lagoon

Blue here is a shell for you
Inside you'll hear a sigh
A foggy lullaby
There is your song from me

—JONI MITCHELL, "Blue," 1970

Late Bloomer

In 1880, after examining the evolution of color terminology in various languages, German philosopher and philologist Lazarus Geiger announced a startling discovery: the great ancient texts of the Indian, Chinese, Jewish, Icelandic, Roman, and Greek civilizations contain no words for the color blue, despite a heavy emphasis in some of these texts on sky and sea. The color blue appears nowhere in Homer's poems—though the descriptive phrase "wine-dark sea" first appeared in the *Iliad*—nor in the Hebrew Bible, nor in the Hindu Vedas. When the ancient Egyptians began to make blue dyes from lapis lazuli, they assigned a word to the color, making them the first civilization to do so. They later produced the first artificial pigment—in approximately 2500 B.C.—a blue known today as Egyptian blue.

Geiger observed that blue was, in every language he studied, the last color to be named and that the other colors were named in a consistent order. His theory that humans evolved the ability to perceive color over the last few millennia has been disproven. But the question still lingers: Can we really "see" a color for which we have no name?

Living with Waterside

The world of Waterside is vast; blues evoke a multitude of moods and associations, depending on hue, shade, and application. But as varied as they are, blues almost always come across as intelligent, honest, and interesting without too much fanfare.

There are some universal blues—in the range of indigo moving toward navy—that just seem to transcend trend and time. These are blues that are easy to incorporate into a decor and easy to live with. They are suitable for all-blue rooms, are dynamic with white, and can be used effortlessly as accents on walls or in upholstery. They work with neutrals, both cool and warm. In fact, they are, to the modern eye, neutrals unto themselves and can be handled with the freedom of hand that other neutrals allow.

In the fabrics I design, I tend to favor inky blues that hint toward teal and the quiet gray-blues. They intrigue me because they are at once calm and turbulent—and they have movement. European clients often tell me that the blues I use resemble the sky when the sun is setting, as opposed to French blue, which captures more of a sunrise. I enjoy these colors in a room where I want to feel grounded.

The lighter aquarelle blues are more spirited, and in a way, spiritual. Like the light sky, they can inspire thoughts beyond the world as we know it, albeit in a gentle and familiar way. Because they relate to the outdoors, they are naturally beautiful and evocative as a ceiling color or any focal point in which we might seek the effect of distance. They are not anchoring colors—they have the opposite effect, of unmooring the eye—and should be combined with defining colors to delineate spaces.

For the most intimate environments, I choose the quiet light blues, the ones with a good measure of cream or gray in them. I recommend them highly for the bedroom, as they are the shades that make a bedroom a sanctuary. They provide a transition, a way to move between our day lives and sleep. They are peaceful, forgiving, and gentle, the stuff of sweet dreams.

The bathroom is the perfect place to use soft and midtone blues reminiscent of the sea and sky. Stone tiles or slabs of various quartzites, especially when they are honed, look and feel natural, and the honing makes them less slippery. Slab material on vanity tops feels more expansive—making a small bathroom appear larger. And blue glass tiles are lovely and reflective if you want more shimmer. If you are unable to use tile or stone, choose a wonderful watery blue paint for the walls, combined with a crisp white or cream trim and ceiling color for contrast.

... The sky o'erarches here,
we feel the undulating deck
beneath our feet,
We feel the long pulsation,
ebb and flow of endless
motion,
The tones of unseen
mystery, the vague and
vast suggestions of the
briny world,
the liquid-flowing syllables,
The perfume, the faint
creaking of the cordage,
the melancholy rhythm,
The boundless vista and
the horizon far and dim
are all here,
And this is ocean's poem.

—WALT WHITMAN, "In Cabin'd Ships
at Sea," from *Leaves of Grass*, 1870

Indigo Thumbprint

Levi Strauss was operating a San Francisco dry goods business in 1872 when he received a letter from Jacob Davis, a tailor in Reno, Nevada, describing how he used copper rivets to fortify the work pants he made for his customers. Davis wanted to patent the riveting process and suggested that Strauss, from whom Davis purchased fabric, join him in procuring the patent. Strauss agreed, and in May 1873 the patent for riveting pants was granted to them.

Davis moved to San Francisco to oversee the manufacturing of the pants, known at the time as "waist overalls," which Levi Strauss & Company offered in both cotton duck and blue denim, a durable cotton twill. The first such denim pant was known enigmatically as "XX," the name of the fabric used to make it. It wasn't until around 1890 that the garment came to be called by the product lot number the company assigned to it: 501.

Blue jeans weren't worn widely by the masses until after World War II, when they became the clothing of choice for both real-life and on-screen rebels, like James Dean (and as Jim Stark in *Rebel Without a Cause*) and Marlon Brando (as Terry Malloy in *On the Waterfront*). "Hollywood costume designers put all the bad boys in denim," according to former Strauss archivist Lynn Downey. Efforts to ban blue jeans in schools only fanned teenage desire for them, particularly after twenty-four-year-old Dean's death in a 1955 car crash. In the 1960s, a decade of much political unrest and cultural change, jeans became the democratizing uniform of a generation committed to class and gender equality, and not long after, of the rest of the world.

The blue jean is ubiquitous, yet is one of the most highly personal clothing items, and for two main reasons: first, jeans tend to acquire the shape of the wearer over time, and, second, the indigo in which they are dyed sits on top of the denim fibers, rather than in them, which results in the legendary tendency to fade to different degrees and in different patterns for each person. Or as Paul Trynka, author of *Denim: From Cowboys to Catwalks*, puts it, "[t]he eternal appeal of jeans is just that they reflect us and they reflect the lives that we've had in them"—like an indigo diary.

"I want to die with my blue jeans on."

—ANDY WARHOL, from *The Philosophy of Andy Warhol (From A to B & Back Again)*, 1975

A Blue Room

Blue is a tremendously versatile color, as it clashes with few other colors and can be used to harmonize other diverse color groups. But when contemplating what shade or shades of blue to use in an interior, especially on walls, consider how you plan to use the room.

Here are some guidelines.

- Lighter Blues: Lighter shades create a tranquil environment and make a room feel more spacious. Cooler shades are best suited to rooms that receive an abundance of natural light; the warm glow of the sun provides a good counterbalance.
- Midtone Blues: These are the most versatile shades of blue, as they are easy on the eye and compatible with a range of furnishing styles. If you want to create a country look, a slightly grayed blue is a good choice. The more greenish blues in midtone values, like those associated with the Caribbean, change the most in response to changes in light, a quality that creates more depth and interest. As for the sky blues, which are between the light and midtones, they are uplifting and restful at the same time.
- Darker Blues: Dark shades of blue like indigo are serious, moody, and dramatic. Use them when you want more atmosphere. Dark blues like navy create a crisp, nautical look when combined with bright white molding, and a more classic look when combined with cream molding. For intense drama, keep the moldings the same blue. With these darker blues, it is good to use lower light levels. That may seem counterintuitive, but low lights will define the room's parameters, making the color feel less endless.
- Bright Blues: These power blues are energetic and add a punch to whatever decor they are coordinating with. They add a very contemporary twist to what can otherwise be more classic. Ultramarine is a great choice for a modern look and can also be used as an accent wall.

"The deeper blue becomes, the more urgently it summons man toward the infinite, the more it arouses in him a longing for purity and, ultimately, for the supersensual."

—WASSILY KANDINSKY, *Concerning the Spiritual in Art*, 1911

Little Girl Blue

So accustomed are many cultures to the color-coded world of babies—namely, blue is for boys, pink is for girls, at least in North America—one might assume this practice has a pedigree. It doesn't. Babies and young children of both sexes generally wore white dresses until pastel-colored children's clothing became available in the mid-1800s. Even then, according to Jo B. Paoletti, author of *Pink and Blue: Telling the Girls from the Boys in America*, there were no consistent color assignments based on gender until nearly a century later. A 1927 edition of *Time* magazine, for example, published a chart outlining gender-appropriate clothing for girls and boys according to major retailers in the United States; Filene's of Boston, Best & Co. in New York City, and Halle's of Cleveland all advised mothers to dress their boys in pink. It was not until the 1940s that these stores began assigning blue to boys' clothing and pink to girls'—just in time for baby boomers to reject the custom as sexist. The practice reemerged in the mid-1980s, as it became more common for parents-to-be to find out a baby's gender before birth and then shop for clothing according to commercial norms.

Buttoned Up

When the British Royal Navy standardized its officers' uniforms in 1748, it chose a very dark blue for the fabric, and "navy blue," as we know it today, was born. According to legend, King George II selected the color based on the dark-blue-and-white riding habit that the Duchess of Bedford sported on her jaunts through Hyde Park; that the Duke of Bedford was First Lord of the Admiralty during the selection process gives this story a veneer of plausibility. In her book *Nautical Chic*, however, Amber Jane Butchart proposes some less whimsical rationales for the selection, such as the government's access to a steady supply of indigo and the long association between blue and seafaring in England's history (Elizabeth I, for example, distributed blue coats to the English naval forces that battled the Spanish Armada). Either way, the color's association with the Royal Navy, which went on to become the most dominant navy in the world, helped establish it not only as a symbol of competence and authority but also as the color of choice for uniforms in military, law enforcement, and civilian circles.

In 1846, Queen Victoria, apparently smitten with the naval look, began dressing her sons in navy-blue-and-white sailor suits, sparking a trend that spread well beyond the shores of England and lasted until the British Empire waned. Today still, Japanese students, especially the girls, still sport uniforms that reflect the naval influences of that bygone era.

Branded Blue

In 1845, Tiffany & Co. published its first Blue Book, a catalog of its handmade jewelry bound in a cover of robin's egg blue, and the color eventually adorned its boxes, bags, and other promotional materials. The color was selected by founder Charles Lewis Tiffany, who, the company speculates, may have been influenced by the popularity of turquoise gemstones at the time. "Tiffany Blue," as the color is now called, is a private custom hue, Pantone PMS 1837, the number reflecting the year Tiffany founded the company. Tiffany Blue is one of the most recognizable signature colors in the commercial world, and a very glamorous one at that. As Tiffany proudly proclaims on its website, "one glance at this glorious hue evokes not only excitement but also appreciation for a legendary style that was crafted by artisans working in a tradition established more than 175 years ago."

Blue Devotion

Over the centuries, blue has emerged as a deeply meaningful color in Judaism; it is the color on the flag of Israel and the color of Hanukkah. It is also believed to be the color that the Hebrew Bible commands Jews to include in the threads of their tallits, or prayer shawls. Scholar Zvi C. Koren, who specializes in the analytic chemistry of antiquated colorants, entered the debate about the original hue of this biblically mandated blue, called *tekhelet*, when he examined a two-thousand-year-old scrap of fabric—the oldest known sample of the dye salvaged from Masada in 2011. He concluded that, it would have been a deep purple-blue, "the color of the sky at midnight." The formula for the dye, which was made from the secretions of sea snails still found on Israel's beaches, was lost in the years following the Roman destruction of Jerusalem's Second Temple in A.D. 70.

"To most persons, as to myself, the ethereal, suave, transparent timbre of the flute, with its placidity and its poetic charm, produces an auditive sensation analogous to the visual impression of the color blue, a fine blue, pure and luminous as the azure of the sky."

—ALBERT LAVIGNAC, *Music and Musicians*, 1899

Do You See
What I Taste?

When I was six, my parents took me to a performance of the Philharmonic Orchestra at Lincoln Center. I wasn't a fan of classical music, or of any other particular genre, at that point in my life, but it turned out to be an incredible experience. For some reason, I decided to close my eyes, and as the music played, I saw color. I am sure my parents thought I was asleep, but I was very much awake, enjoying a fantastic light show. From that point on, whenever music was on the radio I played a game with myself: name that color. Sometimes I heard monochromatic colors, but more often it was a multitude. Nothing was black and white in my world of synesthesia.

Synesthesia is a neurological phenomenon in which a stimulus in one sense, such as sight, instantly creates a sensation in another sense, such as taste. Literally translated, it means to "perceive together." It has been a subject of interest since antiquity, but until recently science tended to dismiss it as the fanciful product of overly active imaginations. A resurgence of interest in the topic in the late 1980s yielded some astounding findings. The synesthetic experience is observable on brain scans, for example, which can demonstrate when a single stimulus activates multiple regions of the brain associated with the different senses. Studies suggest that all babies are born synesthetic and remain so until six months of age, at which point the senses begin to specialize and separate. That separation process is not completed until around the age of eleven.

No one knows for sure why some people retain synesthetic abilities, nor is it known with any degree of certainty how many of us are synesthetic. Estimates range from one in twenty-three to one in two thousand. Synesthesia appears to run in families: Vladimir Nabokov was a synesthete—as were his mother and son—and wrote about the experience in his autobiography *Speak, Memory*. For Nabokov, every letter of the alphabet had a distinct and consistent color, which is a common expression of synesthesia. He wrote: "In the green group, there are alder-leaf *f*, the unripe apple of *p*, and pistachio *t*. Dull green, combined somehow with violet, is the best I can do for *w*. The yellows comprise various *e*'s and *I*'s, creamy *d*, bright-golden *y*, and *u*, whose alphabetical value I can express only by 'brassy with an olive sheen.'" But there are other forms of synesthesia too, in which music may instantly produce vivid colored shapes; Tuesdays may be green; the baritone voice may sound purple; and steak may taste crimson.

We all have many ways of connecting to color, and we don't have to be synesthetes to do it. But if we took the time to fully experience and examine our sensory responses to the world around us, we just might find the color in the music we hear, the food we eat, and the words we read and write.

"Passing on to the blue group, there is steely x, thundercloud z, and huckleberry h."

—VLADIMIR NABOKOV, *Speak Memory*, 1966

2

Silverlight

Star Quality

In 1972, when David Bowie took to the stage on the British television program *Top of the Pops*, he introduced his alter ego, alien Ziggy Stardust, to fifteen million viewers with a performance of "Starman." His androgynous, space-age, and sexually charged persona may have been an unwelcome jolt to establishment types, but it electrified rock fans and reignited a career that had languished since Bowie's last and only hit song three years earlier, "Space Oddity." Ziggy's futuristic sensibilities and his band's metallic space suits captured the zeitgeist of an era in which man had just walked on the moon, audiences were digesting Stanley Kubrick's *A Space Odyssey*, and children watched *The Jetsons* with their Saturday morning Lucky Charms.

Ziggy did not last long as a stage presence, but Bowie was onto something rather profound. Astrophysicists have known for some time that the universe and every piece of living and nonliving matter within it is made of materials that were forged in stars and released upon their explosion. Theoretical physicist Lawrence Krauss put it most eloquently in his book, *A Universe from Nothing: Why There Is Something Rather Than Nothing*: "One of the most poetic facts I know about the universe is that essentially every atom in your body was once inside a star that exploded. Moreover, the atoms in your left hand probably came from a different star than did those in your right. We are all, literally, star children, and our bodies made of stardust."

It is little wonder that we are so attracted to stars and that we covet their cool, reflective fire. We see that fire in the clean sleekness of silver, the icy beauty of diamonds, the refracted light of crystalline snow, the reflected light of the simple mirror, the clear light of a drop of water, the quicksilver moon, and white lightning.

Dazzling Armor
Steely
Mercury
Aloof
Sleek
Worldly Transcendent
Sterling Cosmic
Nickel
Palladium
Frost Crystalline Oracular
Titanium Mica Chrome
Infinite Sexy Platinum
Pewter Argent Pure
Modern
Aluminum Futuristic

More Than Just
a Pretty Face

Six thousand years: that's the conservative estimate for how long humans have utilized silver's purifying and protective properties. The ancients did not need to know what a bacterium looked like or that silver possessed the remarkable ability to destroy it to understand that their silver bowls and vessels protected them from illness or that silver compounds promoted the healing of wounds and infections. Experience showed them that food and liquids stored in silver containers remained fresher longer, and that wounds treated with silver healed faster. Ancient Egyptians, Phoenicians, Greeks, and Romans used silver vessels for the storage and transport of food and drink, and the Macedonians and Greeks used silver to promote wound healing. In the first millennium A.D., silver was employed to purify blood and treat bad breath, and in the second millennium, it was used in a variety of forms—silver nitrate solutions, creams, and surgical supplies—to prevent and cure skin, eye, and blood infections. Prior to the development of antibiotics in the twentieth century, silver was the most important germ-fighting substance in the world.

A recent resurgence of interest in the metal's protective effects, including nanoscale silver that is a few ten-thousandths the width of human hair, has again pushed silver to the forefront in the fight against disease, especially diseases that are antibiotic resistant. In 2013, researchers at Harvard University found that combining antibiotics with a silver solution made the antibiotics ten to one thousand times more effective against resistant bacteria by weakening their membranes and causing them to produce molecules that damage their DNA. With the development of nanoscale silver, manufacturers were able to embed silver particles in threads, metals, and other materials used to produce medical and consumer products. This technique has been used to make clothing and home appliances that promise to fight germs and odors, such as socks, yoga mats, and washing machines.

Purity never goes out of style.

Living with Silverlight

Silverlight is the celebrity of the color world. It is glamorous, trendy, otherworldly, and forward-looking. Its sleek reflectivity makes everything around it more interesting. Moreover, its dualities—it can be both old and new, traditional and trendy, sleek and ornate, earthbound and extraterrestrial—make it enormously versatile in a room or on a table.

Silverlight requires some handling too. It is best used in measured quantities, against more subtle backdrops that showcase its extraordinary gifts. It is, of course, the color of choice for table accessories and dinnerware. It is used generously in art and lighting fixtures. When designing fabric, I tend to use it as an accessory, too, often in the form of metallic thread, a sequin, or a bead, to bring light and interest to matte materials. Used in small amounts, a Silverlight detail can transform an ordinary fabric or wallcovering into something unique and glamorous. It is this sparkle that brings attention and dimension to the material.

Silver velvet cushions and cool metallic silk drapes add sophistication to living rooms without overwhelming them. A chair upholstered in a cool gray silk taffeta will appear metallic because of the sheen and add drama to complement a matte upholstered sofa fabric, particularly if the sofa is accented with matching silver-toned pillows. Add a pewter holdback for the drapes as an accessory for a polished look.

In dining rooms, upholstered chair backs in pewter metallic faux leather create a sleek, modern look. Velvet fabrics embossed with foil prints are beautiful and versatile, playing on the juxtaposition of the soft and plush texture against high-sheen sleek. They can be used for both furniture and tabletops, especially runners.

There is an exception to the rule of moderation in the use of Silverlight materials, one that I apply when designing wallcoverings. The scale and linear nature of walls, even ceilings, allows for a more generous use of Silverlight-producing materials. Rather than overwhelming these surfaces, Silverlight's presence in wallcoverings looks clean and current. A silver-leaf wallcovering or silver-painted tin ceiling can expand a space and reflect light; in fact, my favorite designs combine handmade artisanal paper made from recycled materials with silver leaf or a silver print on top. The combination of rough and polished materials is dynamic. Imperfections in the handmade paper only increase this impression and make us feel more comfortable. In my collection of handmade wallcoverings, the papers are usually rough, tactile, and relatable to nature. The silver leaf evokes luxury and elegance. The combination is a balance of livability and statement.

Slowly, silently, now the moon
Walks the night in her silver shoon;
This way, and that, she peers, and sees
Silver fruit upon silver trees;
One by one the casements catch
Her beams beneath the silvery thatch;
Couched in his kennel, like a log,
With paws of silver sleeps the dog;
From their shadowy cote the white breasts peep
Of doves in a silver-feathered sleep;
A harvest mouse goes scampering by,
With silver claws, and silver eye;
And moveless fish in the water gleam,
By silver reeds in a silver stream.

—WALTER DE LA MARE, "Silver," from *Peacock Pie: A Book of Rhymes*, 1913

The Mighty Web

Ounce for ounce, spider silk has five times the tensile strength—the ability to withstand breakage under tension—of steel, and scientists have been studying its molecular structure in hopes of replicating it in synthetic silk thread. The potential uses for spider silk are many and varied: surgical sutures, paper products, air bags, parachutes, protective clothing, nets, and rope. So strong is spider silk that the Pentagon has investigated its use in body armor.

Spider silk is hard to come by, however. In 2008, weavers in Madagascar completed an eleven-by-four-foot tapestry entirely of spider silk, an effort that took four years of labor and the output of more than one million golden orb spiders to pull it off.

Efforts to harvest spider silk in more significant quantities have led scientists to crossbreed spiders with goats, whose milk contains a protein that can be extracted and woven into spider silk thread. That thread has been incorporated into a fabric that, in 2012, Dutch scientists cultured with human skin cells that grew to cover the silk over the course of five weeks. In laboratory tests, the resulting silk skin was able to withstand penetration by a bullet moving at half the speed (179 yards or 164 meters per second) of a .22-caliber rifle shot, but not one shot at full speed, the standard for bulletproof vests. Further improvements may one day yield viable bulletproof vests made of the silk.

Glass Light Treatments

The glass we use in the fixtures that light a home impart a definitive interior design statement. Cut glass makes for a more classic, traditional look, while blown glass makes for a more contemporary one. Crystal glass lends itself to a more ornate interior, and, one of my favorites, rock crystal, throws off a more organic vibe. Dimmers and choice of bulbs are important too: dimmers are a must to control the brightness of a room, and bulbs are critical to suggesting a feeling of warmth or coolness.

Mirror, Mirror

Reflective, expansive, even magical, mirrors are a vital part of the Silverlight color world. Using reflective materials in interiors is one of the most effective ways to make a space look larger and bring light into a room. Place mirrors in a narrow hallway, on the back of a bookcase, or on a dining room wall to enlarge a space. You can also use large mirrors in small spaces; the combination is sophisticated and dramatic. Mercury mirrors add interest with their dappled surfaces, and they work in both modern and traditional spaces.

Art-deco-inspired mirrored furniture has a timeless elegance and great versatility too. Vanities, hallway tables, and side tables wear this style particularly well, and like wall mirrors, they add light to interiors. Use a piece in any room of the home that you want to dress up.

Ice is becoming itself
Random crystal clusters
Origami trees silhouetted
Against the last light

—MARY MacGOWAN, "Untitled," 2012

Snow's Secrets

For most of us, "snow" is just "snow." But for some of the world's northernmost populations, who live in and around snow for much of the year, the vocabulary relating to those silver-white flakes is a good deal more nuanced.

In 2010, a team of researchers led by anthropologist Igor Krupnik of the Smithsonian Arctic Studies Center completed a study of certain Eskimo dialects and determined that they contain many more words for snow than the English language, a phenomenon first observed by Franz Boas in his 1911 book *Handbook of American Indian Languages*. Some linguists came to regard Boas's report as apocryphal, questioning its accuracy and the subsequent scholarship based on it. Krupnik's study, however, supports Boas's observations. In it, one dialect, the Yupik, was found to contain ten words for snow; the Inuit was reported to contain at least fifty-three. Among them are words that connote snow that is good for travel by sled, snow that is powdery crystals, and snow that is softly falling.

There is a great deal of utility in this arsenal of terms—"a matter of life and death"— for people who live in snowy climates. There is a great deal of artistry in it too: so much of art, after all, is born of keen observation and study. As Thoreau wrote in his journal (August 5, 1851), "The question is not what you look at, but what you see."

If you look at something long enough, it just might begin to tell you its secrets.

"Big girls love big diamonds."

—ELIZABETH TAYLOR

The Regent Diamond

There are scores of named diamonds, each with its own legend. Many have seen war; others murder; some have journeyed through weddings, beheadings, and coronations. The Regent diamond is said to have done it all. Originally 426 uncut carats, it was discovered in 1701 in the Parteal mine in Central India by a native mine laborer, a member of the servile Sudra caste. It is said that the Sudra cut his own leg in order to hide the stone in the wound or under thick bandages he applied, after which he escaped to Machilipatnam on the Bay of Bengal, where he met an English skipper to whom he offered the stone in exchange for transporting him to freedom. The skipper allowed the Sudra on board, where he took possession of the stone and threw the man overboard to his death. The skipper sold the stone to an Indian merchant named Jamchund, who then resold it to Thomas Pitt, governor of Fort St. George in Madras, India.

Pitt arranged for the stone, now called the "Pitt diamond," to be cut in London, which took two years. The result was a 141-carat brilliant-cut diamond and several smaller-cut diamonds, the latter of which were purchased by Russian tsar Peter the Great. Despite his honorable dealings, Pitt was accused of having acquired the stone through treachery, damaging both his reputation and peace of mind. In 1717, he sold the diamond to the Duke of Orleans, regent of France, at which point it became known as the Regent diamond.

The stone graced the crown of Louis XV at his coronation in 1722, after which he took to wearing the stone in his hat. Louis XVI also wore the Regent in his crown for his coronation in 1775, and thereafter on his hat too. His queen, Marie Antoinette, also adorned herself with the diamond, once in a spray of feathers attached to a black hat for a costume ball.

In 1792, in the chaos of the French Revolution, the Regent, along with other of the crown jewels, was stolen from the Garde-Meuble, but it was recovered a year later from among the timbers of a roof, the same year Louis XVI and Marie Antoinette were beheaded. Napoleon Bonaparte subsequently used it to embellish his sword when he was first consul and again in his double sword in 1812, as emperor. When the monarchy returned to power in France, the Regent was there too, in the crowns of Louis XVIII, Charles X, Napoleon III, and in the Grecian diadem of his wife, Empress Eugenie.

In 1870, the Bank of France took custody of the crown jewels, including the Regent, and shipped them to Brest for safekeeping. The jewels were placed in the hold of a ship after France entered into an armistice with Germany in 1871 and remained there until 1872, when they were returned to Paris and deposited with the Ministry of Finance. In 1882, the National Assembly voted to sell many of the crown jewels but decided to preserve the Regent, and a few other pieces, in the Louvre, where it still rests.

Expecto Patronum

The Patronus that saves Harry Potter from the Dementors in *The Prisoner of Azkaban* appears as a stag—beautiful, graceful, noble. Like all the Patronuses we meet in the Harry Potter series, this one is silver and emits a brilliant silver light. Conjured from the happiest memories that a person can muster, and in some cases, connected intimately to those its conjurer loves most, the silver Patronus is an ingenious symbol of protection and refuge against the darkness of despair.

I know what it is to need a Patronus—and to have one. Mine, although not as artful as those in the Harry Potter series, is silver too.

My father passed away at eighty-seven, and while he was quite old, I did not expect it. He was in the hospital for a relatively minor procedure, and I visited him the evening before he died. I was never close with my father. No one was, really. He was a gentleman and a scholar, but inaccessible to just about everyone.

But that evening, he talked and talked and talked—more than he had in our entire life together. He talked about his life, his experiences in World War II, his love for my mother, his time on earth. In retrospect, I realize he was preparing to leave us.

I was there next to him the following day when his heart stopped. I started to cry, and I told my father I loved him, something I had never been able to say to him easily. I was frightened, really frightened, to find myself standing at the crossroads between my father's life and his death, watching him go.

But here's what I really want to tell you, as hard as it is to describe: at that moment of fear and grief, in that room, silver was everywhere around me, permeating everything, including me and my father. I began to breathe deeply, and it was silver I was breathing. Cleansing, purifying silver. Whether the angels brought it, or whether that silver was a call to them, they came and took my dad. The road they traveled was Silverlight.

My memories of my father have become peaceful ones. Now, when I am afraid, I breathe silver. It has never failed me.

"And then, through the fog that was drowning him, he thought he saw a silvery light grow brighter and brighter.... The blinding light was illuminating the grass around him.... The screaming had stopped, the cold was ebbing away..."

—J. K. ROWLING, *Harry Potter and the Prisoner of Azkaban*, 1999

3

Garden Party

Easter Parade

As a girl, I loved celebrations of all kinds. But as a Jewish girl growing up outside New York City, there were a few major ones that were off-limits to me under my family's regime. Christmas was one of them, with its jingle bells and pine and colored lights. On the sly, I would join a friend and his family to trim their tree, working my hand at the forbidden arts of ornament hanging, tinsel draping, and popcorn stringing, all the while serenaded by Christmas songs both sacred and worldly. These things held no religious significance to me; they were purely aesthetic, and if I felt a pang of remorse as I lit the menorah later at home, I don't remember it now.

But no holiday stirred a deeper longing in me than Easter. Arriving just as spring began to deliver on its promise of warmth and vibrant new greens, the Easter holiday generated a spectacle of color that captivated me with its whimsical exuberance, drawing me away from the grays and browns of late winter. Hyacinth blue, pale yellow, powder pink and rose pink, Creamsicle orange, mint green, lavender, buttercream—all the beautiful pastels seemed to bloom suddenly in department store window displays and in the form of artificial flowers on mannequins, overflowed in the form of foil-wrapped eggs and jelly beans on candy counters everywhere, and popped up in fashion advertisements and magazines.

It was as if these colors demanded a shift in perspective and mood, a letting go, a lightening up. They reached their apogee in New York City's traditional Easter Parade, which still runs on Fifth Avenue. There, otherwise seemingly sensible women wear bonnets ornamented with towering flowers, and occasional eggs and live chicks, in spring's playful palette. Men dare to wear top hats and to accent themselves in powdery colors while walking alongside six-foot-tall pink-and-white rabbits. Fittingly, the parade originated spontaneously in the 1870s, when elite families, attired in their Easter Sunday finery, gathered after church services. Over the years, attendance at this widely-anticipated event has grown enormously, drawing in regular folks as well as celebrities.

Passover notwithstanding, I wanted in. My parents still refused to take me to the parade, but I found opportunities to decorate eggs with my friends, becoming the undisputed expert in creating elaborate plaids and stripes and polka-dot patterns in those distinctive pastel dyes that the Paas tablets yielded with vinegar and water. When I was old enough to go into the city alone, I went to a Ukrainian church gift shop and bought a warmed-wax dispenser so I could create dye-resistant designs, the same tool and the same technique I later used to embellish the hand-painted scarves with which I launched my career.

The joy, youth, and lightness of these springtime colors were their own world, one in which nonsense was welcome and worry was not. As adults, we shy away from them somewhat for their lack of intensity and gravitas. But therein lies their magic.

10-1420
Spring

Charming
Pink
Wisteria
Open
Impish
Peach
Curious
Celadon
Whimsical
Warmhearted
Funny
Cantaloupe
Spirited
Childlike
Joyous
Positive
Lichen
Magnolia
Lettuce
Lilac
Naive
Spontaneous
Lemongrass
Buttercup
Lavender
Imaginative
Powder blue
Coral

Revel Without a Cause

In the Disney film *Mary Poppins*, there's a scene where Mary and Bert—with the Banks children in tow—visit Uncle Albert. The first time we see Uncle Albert, he is floating up near the ceiling, laughing uncontrollably. His laughter is so contagious that Bert and the children soon begin to laugh with him, at which point they too ascend to the ceiling, where they all bob like balloons, giggling, snickering, and howling, until sad thoughts bring them back to earth again. It is the characters' laughter that gives them levity, not the other way around. The laughter comes first.

Few of us need science to tell us that laughing makes us feel good, but science does tell us that. The pleasant release of muscle tension, elevated mood, changed outlook, diminution of pain—all these are rooted in our physiological reactions to laughter, and they are predictable and powerful enough that their therapeutic value is recognized even among practitioners of traditional Western medicine.

When my youngest daughter, Sophie, was in her first years of elementary school, she would launch into an astonishing and hilarious comedy routine that defied the domestic order I craved and tried to foster at the precise time she should've been preparing for bed. She monkeyed, mocked, swang, sang, impersonated, parroted, laughed, and danced. This was not a gradual thing; her humor emerged all at once, intensely sunny, bright, fully formed—from where I knew not. I usually could withstand its effects for the first couple of minutes—I believe strongly in the importance of bedtimes—but inevitably her luminosity, as bright and yellow as the sun, made me crack. I moved from a stifled smile to a stifled giggle to full-on laughter, and who can stifle that? May we all fill our lives with yellow.

"A little nonsense now and then is cherished by the wisest men."

—ROALD DAHL, *Charlie and the Great Glass Elevator*, 1972

Salon de Thé

After a fire destroyed his Parisian bakery in 1871, Louis Ernest Ladurée decided to rebuild it as a pastry shop. He chose Jules Cheret, renowned painter and poster artist, to decorate it. Cheret selected a rich celadon as the shop's primary color and, with the decor of the Palais Garnier as his inspiration, embellished its ceilings with images of cherubs, albeit dressed as pastry chefs. Cheret's handiwork made Ladurée as famous for its elegant interior as for its pastries.

At the time, the city's bustling café culture was primarily the province of men, so when Ladurée incorporated a tearoom into its shop a few years following its opening, it was a revolutionary move that gave women a public space in which to socialize and talk about the affairs of the day while partaking of various pastries and tea. With the opening of its *salon de thé*, Ladurée became not just a purveyor of delicious treats but also of an experience.

It was not until the middle of the twentieth century, however, that the patisserie introduced its now-famous macaron composed of two delicate meringue cookie shells with a ganache filling. The appearance of macarons in Ladurée's windows and display cases added a showstopping profusion of color to its sumptuous decor. Today still, towering trays of these confections in varying shades of pink, green, yellow, purple, beige, and brown hint at their exquisite flavors. A pale hue of creamy orange marks the orange blossom macaron; a distinctive spring green, the lime basil; and an elegant petal pink, the rose raspberry ginger. Displayed against Ladurée's traditional celadon green interior, alongside its rows of assorted French pastries and other sweets, the macarons are the stars in this celebration of the senses.

Living with Garden Party Colors

The colors of spring—pastels mixed with the greens of new grass—are inherently joyful, hopeful, and youthful. Their gentleness makes them suitable for children's rooms (peruse any catalog for children's furnishings and you will see lots of these colors), and their freshness makes them appropriate for any rooms in which we want a subtle exuberance.

Apricot, pale blue, soft greens, and corals are all lovely in interior spaces, but they must be used in the right combination, or the result can be cloying or garish. When working with large surfaces, like rugs, walls, or sofas, pick two colors, either warm or cool, but not one of each, from the Garden Party palette. In other words, from the same side of the color wheel. Celery green and powder blue work together, for example, as do coral and apricot. Multicolored prints and patterns featuring the spectrum of Garden Party colors can be added against this backdrop in smaller applications, such as pillows and bedding.

Mixing neutrals with pastels, for example, cream-colored moldings against a lavender wall, adds a softness and sophistication to them, while using a crisp white molding against pastels creates a youthful look. I don't recommend combining pastels with darker tones, as it takes the joy out of them.

These colors are best used in measured doses; as accents, they work particularly well: pillows, throw blankets, table runners and other linens, baskets, picture frames, and lampshades are all good choices.

An easy, effective, albeit obvious, way to bring the palette into your home is with flowers. Freshly cut flowers are a way to bring the outside in year-round, and in the winter months, surrounding ourselves with Garden Party colors keeps our spirits high.

"Life is a combination of magic and pasta."

—FEDERICO FELLINI, from *I, Fellini*, 2001

A Leap of Faith

In the early 1990s, when I was designing textiles for Larsen, I approached the National Dance Institute, Jacques d'Amboise's organization dedicated to exposing schoolchildren to the art form, with a proposal to create a collection based on its students' visual interpretations of music. The Institute generously accommodated me, and for one full week, in a tarp-filled studio, the young dancers translated music of all genres and tempos that I had selected for them—from Vivaldi and jazz to aboriginal melodies—into paintings and sketches. The kids were exuberant, uninhibited, natural artists and supplied me with hundreds of incredible works.

I couldn't be sure that these young artists would respond to the music, let alone with joyous abandon, or whether their work could be translated into fabric design, but the experiment was a success. We curated their art into a fabric collection called "Rhythm and Line." It sold well, generated royalties for the Institute, garnered a number of design awards, and has been written about and exhibited in museums. The experience was not only an affirmation of the great beauty of taking a leap of creative faith and diving in, of relinquishing control, of being present and just doing, but a reminder that doing so can result in greater creativity, successful work, and pure joy.

Light As Astaire

The plot may be thin, the acting unexceptional at times, and the songs occasionally formulaic, but there is nothing in the world like a Fred Astaire movie. Even in black-and-white and without modern stereo sound, these works are transporting. We are buoyed by the seamless fantasy of Astaire's ingenious dance on the ceiling in *Royal Wedding*; wooed by the elegant, romantic intensity of his "Cheek to Cheek" duet with Ginger Rogers in *Top Hat*; and awed by his impossible drum and tap solo in *Damsel in Distress*.

Weaving Astaire's graceful, expressive, seemingly effortless movement into whimsical tales of love and courtship, his films are gorgeous tapestries whose lightness, even frivolity, at times seems incongruous with the enormity and rarity of his talent. Today, Astaire remains the most admired dancer among the world's most admired dancers, past and present. Choreographers George Balanchine and Jerome Robbins cited him as their greatest influence. Rudolf Nureyev wanted to move like him. Mikhail Baryshnikov did too: when asked why so many dancers talk about Astaire, he answered simply, "unmatched perfection."

"All [Fred Astaire] did was sing and dance with greater craft and feeling than anyone in movie history."

—RICHARD CORLISS, *Time*, February 1, 2010

Sorbet Stories

Sorbet is among the simplest of food—usually composed of ice, sugar, and flavoring, often from pulped fruit—but it has attracted our admiration for centuries, as a dessert, as a palate cleanser, and as a refresher in the heat of a summer's day. Its lemon yellows, strawberry pinks, and lime greens are pleasing to the eye, and its pure flavors and aromas, undiluted by milk and cream, focus our senses in a most delightful way.

The origins of sorbet are difficult to pinpoint, wrapped up as they are in myth, as well as the histories of ice cream and other frozen treats. According to one story, the Roman emperor Nero had a hand in the development of sorbet by sending slaves to retrieve snow from the mountains, which he then used to freeze drinks sweetened with honey. Another myth has Marco Polo returning from Asia with the idea of making "ices" (as well as the recipe for pasta), which he allegedly sampled there. And Catherine de' Medici is often credited with popularizing sorbet in Europe when she arrived in France in 1533 to marry the Duke of Orleans.

In their book, *Italian Cuisine: A Cultural History*, Alberto Capatti and Massimo Montanari trace the origins of sorbet to methods of chilling drinks with ice or snow, which had spread throughout Italy by the second half of the sixteenth century. Sorbet emerged from experiments with these drinks and became available in the shops of Naples and Venice by the middle of the seventeenth century. Some of the first known recipes for sorbet were published at the end of the 1600s in a book by Antonio Latini, steward to the Spanish prime minister in Naples. In it he also describes a "milk sorbet," which Capatti and Montanari suggest we might rightfully regard as "the birth certificate of ice cream."

Greens for Your Kitchen

There are few spaces for which I would recommend a spring green or aqua interior, but the kitchen is one of them. Fresh greens are rejuvenating and transformative, as they relate directly to new plant growth and to healthful eating. To that end, an accent wall or backsplash in mint green can freshen a kitchen, especially in urban homes. Green accent pieces—kettles, enameled pots and pans, dishware—allow for an infusion of color that can be changed at a whim. But the easiest, and most natural, way to add green to the kitchen is with real plants and herbs—basil, thyme, rosemary, and mint are good choices—placed where you can smell them.

Practical Magic

One of the first greens to arrive in spring and one of the last to depart at summer's end, mint is among the most popular and versatile herbs on earth and a Merlin among plants. It is both a coolant and a warming agent, a stimulant and a relaxant. It is a traditional flavor in sweets, desserts, and gum but is equally adept at enhancing savory dishes. It stars in cocktails, soft drinks, tea, and liqueur as well as in jelly, ices, and gelato. It is a common ingredient in health and household goods—toothpaste, cold remedies, skin cream, digestive aids, cleaning products, and bug spray—and a featured fragrance in high-end perfume, candles, and spa products.

Named for the Greek nymph Menthe, whose love affair with Hades prompted his jealous wife, Persephone, to turn her into a plant, mint has been a staple in cuisines and

medicines for millennia. Its secret is simple: it makes us feel good. Its exuberant freshness elevates our mood, boosts our alertness, and motivates us while soothing frazzled nerves. Its essential oils increase circulation and decrease inflammation, ameliorating a number of maladies and stresses, both big and small. However you partake of mint, know there is magic in its leaves.

She wore her yellow sun-bonnet,
She wore her greenest gown;
She turned to the south wind
And curtsied up and down.
She turned to the sunlight
And shook her yellow head,
And whispered to her neighbor:
"Winter is dead."

—A.A. MILNE, "Daffodowndilly," 1924

4

Night Shadows

Gotham

Home of comic book hero Batman, Gotham is fictional only to those who have never explored New York City at night. Dusk brings about a transformation of the sharp lines and angles that characterize the city's imposing structures during the daylight hours, softening them, blurring them, sometimes making them invisible at their highest elevations, even making them disappear altogether when the fog rolls in. The colors of the cityscape deepen to their bass notes—dark browns, deep smoky grays, rich charcoals, and inky purples. Outside the spheres of illumination generated by streetlamps and headlights, the things and people of the city can be known only by their darkened silhouettes or the shadows they cast.

These shadows have substance. There is some danger in them, to be sure. They hold secrets and breed intrigue, even scandal. They are full of temptation. But there is opportunity in them too. They promise romance and pleasure, test our powers of interpretation, require us to feel our way, and provide a freeing anonymity.

Author and mythologist Joseph Campbell believed that what we are all seeking, what "it's all finally about," is to "feel the rapture of being alive." Night, with all its colors, invites us to take risks, surrender some control, find rapture, and surprise ourselves.

Merlot
Ambiguous
Subdued
Evocative
Licorice
Raven
Stone
Mysterious
Searching
Masculine
Smoke
Fog
Transformative
Midnight
Cacao
Protective
Secretive
Slate
Sophisticated
Gunmetal
Urban
Sable
Charcoal
Imposing
Shale
Reserved
Espresso
Mahogany
Onyx
Ebony
Sensuous

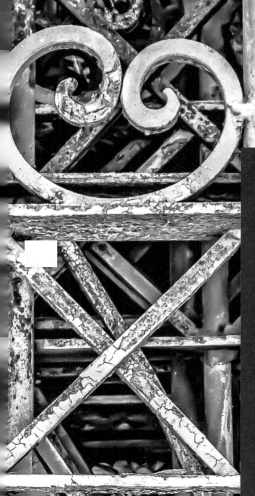

Winged Night

In Greek mythology, there are gods and there are Gods. Nyx, the black-winged Goddess of the Night, falls squarely into the second category. By some accounts, she was born of Chaos, the primeval void before creation, and was among the first deities to exist. By other accounts, she was more at the center of creation; having been courted by the Wind, she laid a silver egg in the womb of darkness from which Eros hatched. By all accounts, she possessed such power and beauty that even the king of the gods, Zeus, feared her and never challenged her, even when they were at cross-purposes. Nyx is portrayed in ancient myth as an oracle and adviser and, of course, the force that rides the sky trailing the veil of night behind her. She lives in the shadows and is never seen in full—only in glimpses.

Nyx bore many powerful children, including Sleep, Day, Fate, Dreams, Old Age, and Death. According to Hesiod's *Theogeny*, she lived in the underworld near the edge of the universe and shared her mansion, but never her time, with her daughter, Day.

Tailored

Decorating with fabrics traditionally associated with menswear creates a classic, timeless look. You can upholster walls or furniture with wool and wool blends in pinstripes and tweeds. If you want to introduce pattern into the mix, layer argyle, herringbone, and houndstooth motifs, which evoke bespoke tailoring and create a dignified sensibility. These fabrics enhance a number of styles; they work with modern and traditional interiors as well as rustic ones.

Gray flannel is a popular menswear fabric for interiors, and for good reason. It is extremely sturdy, usually made of wool (although sometimes combined with other fibers), and it is soft to the touch due to its brushed surface. Use it as a wallcovering for a library or den to add intimacy. Mix it with finishes that are shiny and modern to keep it fresh.

If you use these fabrics in a living room, incorporate bigger, more substantial furniture pieces to go with them. A large coffee table with solid lines, for example, will anchor the room. Bringing in materials like tortoiseshell, bone, or horn in accessories and sculpture complements the menswear sensibility.

Thou knowest the mask of night is on my face;
Else would a maiden blush bepaint my cheek
For that which thou hast heard me speak to-night.

—WILLIAM SHAKESPEARE, *Romeo and Juliet*, Act II, Scene II

Love in the Shadows

Romeo and Juliet's romance is not merely one of young love but also of forbidden love, and night plays a central role in the events that unfold to their tragic, if inevitable, conclusion. Night fires their passion, emboldens their words and actions, and conceals their illicit love from disapproving eyes and enemies. In some of the play's—and literature's—most famous passages, night bears witness to the birth, consummation, and death of their relationship, and figures prominently in the rapturous beauty of Shakespeare's dialogue.

The play is so readily imitated, parodied, and borrowed from that it is easy to forget the power its innocent sensuality exerts over readers and audiences, particularly its nocturnal love scenes. In his acclaimed 1998 book, *Shakespeare: The Invention of the Human*, Harold Bloom described *Romeo and Juliet* as "the largest and most persuasive celebration of romantic love in Western literature," fully deserving of its popularity. And when he thought of the play, he wrote, his mind went directly to its "vital center," that balcony scene, "with its incandescent exchange between the lovers."

OPEN the door now.
Go roll up the collar of your coat
To walk in the changing scarf of mist.

Tell your sins here to the pearl fog
And know for once a deepening night
Strange as the half-meanings
Alurk in a wise woman's mousey eyes.

Yes, tell your sins
And know how careless a pearl fog is

Of the laws you have broken.

—CARL SANDBURG, "Pearl Fog," *The Chicago Poems*, 1916

The Power of
Black and White

Black–and–white photography is very traditional, yet its simplicity lends a spare, eternally modern quality that makes it work with every type of decor.

Display black-and-white images in ways that underscore their tones. Many people use white mats and black frames, but I strongly prefer a white mat and a white frame because white allows the nuances and shadows to present themselves to greatest effect. Arranged on a wall in a neat rectangle or square, frames of different sizes can form a very compelling composition, as can, say, a series of three similarly framed photographs hung vertically or horizontally. Usually it's best not to hang a small image alone on a wall, but doing so can be charming at the end of a narrow hall or nook. Finally, black–and–white images look best displayed together; mixing them with color photographs undercuts the subtlety of their tones.

Veiled Meaning

Since ancient times veils have been among the most ubiquitous and powerful metaphors in art and literature as well as a sartorial reality in the daily lives of millions of women worldwide. Veils obscure, protect, and convey. Yet their connotation can be difficult to interpret, be it to express modesty, reverence, subjugation, purity, or grief, to camouflage identity or one's true intent, or to lend an air of mystery to a fashion look.

The widow's veil of the Victorian era is a fascinating study in such ambiguity. As part of the mourning dress habitually worn by European and American widows of the era, it signified grief and remembrance and provided privacy. But it had other connotations too. According to Harold Koda, former curator in charge of the Costume Institute at New York's Metropolitan Museum of Art, "The veiled widow could elicit sympathy as well as predatory male advances. As a woman of sexual experience without marital constraints, she was often imagined as a potential threat to the social order."

Mourning etiquette at the time allowed for widows to emerge gradually from their black veils and lusterless dresses into lighter shades of subdued color, such as gray and mauve, an outward manifestation of their ebbing grief. But not everyone welcomed the transition to lighter hues. Black became an increasingly popular color for women's fashion in the second half of the nineteenth century, despite, or perhaps because of, its continued association with widows. The 1855 etiquette manual *The Illustrated Manners Book* observed that "[b]lack is becoming, and young widows, fair, plump and smiling, with their roguish eyes sparkling under their black veils are very seducing."

Mourning etiquette began gradually to become less rigid in the last decade of the nineteenth century. By the end of World War I, with its steep and widespread casualties, elaborate mourning attire and prolonged veiling had come to be regarded as impractical and incongruent with the changing role of women in society. In June 1922, *Vogue* detailed some of these changes, noting that widows in the United States rarely wore long crepe veils for more than a year.

Although far less commonly worn today, the widow's veil still has a powerful mystique. Jacqueline Kennedy was so memorable in the black suit and heavy veil she wore to her husband's funeral in 1963 that the *New York Times* mentioned the outfit in her obituary when she died in 1994. Daphne Guinness wore a widow's veil to different effect at the 2010 funeral for Alexander McQueen. Paired with a voluminous black cloak and platform shoes, the veil completed what *New York* magazine called "the most dramatic outfit" at the service, an unorthodox blend of traditional and modern mourning attire to honor a fashion luminary.

"The black moment is the moment when the real message of transformation is going to come."

—JOSEPH CAMPBELL, *The Power of Myth*, 1988

A Cool, Dark Place

My first job out of college was at a major textiles manufacturing firm, where I created floral fabric designs that bore no relation to my artistic aspirations or abilities. Having been advised that my original work was too contemporary for American tastes, I gave up my job, my rent-controlled apartment in New York City, and my boyfriend, and headed to a trade show in Lille, France, with forty-eight original designs in hand. I sold all of them in three days. Heartened by my success and with the proceeds from those sales, I moved to Milan, the epicenter of the design industry, and lived alone there in a friend's apartment.

What happened in Milan? Nothing and everything. I worked on my own creations, but I was alone, and lonely, for the duration of my yearlong residency there. I talked to no one, except while discussing my work (in English) and purchasing the ingredients for my home-cooked dinners (in very bad Italian). What I did, mostly, was walk, particularly in the evenings. Map in hand, I traveled the shadowed streets of Milan by foot with nowhere to go. But, really, there was no map for where I was headed. There was only me.

One day, I was done. That is not an elegant word, but it is accurate. I was finished with Milan and knew it with complete certainty. I called a business contact in Switzerland, who, by some miracle, hired me on the phone. A few weeks later I embarked on the most beautiful train ride of my life into the Alps, the light, and my future.

For years I regarded my time in Milan as something of a lost year, before I finally understood that it was a period of transformation, unbeknownst to me. I had left behind a well-marked path and I needed to develop the strength and self-awareness to find my way. Cloistered in my small world there, I was becoming myself, the grown-up version. Sometimes we need to spend time in the dark to see things clearly.

Serious Living

The colors that compose the world of Night Shadows are masculine, serious, and sophisticated; they are reserved and neutral despite their intensity, encouraging introspection. Charcoal, smoke, ebony, espresso, and even deep burgundy are all part of the Night Shadows world.

If you live in a city, you can create a transition from the outdoors to your living environment by infusing some of the colors of the cityscape. A floor in a rich, dark chocolate stain is an effective way to do that; it's also a good way to anchor a space and provide the foundation from which all else can be showcased. With a dark floor, art, accessories, furniture, and rugs show to full effect without diminishing a sense of order in the room.

Accent walls in shades of night are a sophisticated alternative or addition to dark floors. They contain and protect the interior space in a way that encourages intimacy without overwhelming the senses. But be mindful of their impact; these colors sharpen details and introduce a certain formality to a space. They add depth and, although I prefer the matte finishes, the glossy finishes offer a reflective quality that provides a more

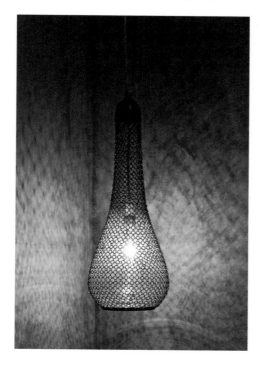

"industrial" feel. Painting an entire room a dark color need not be depressing. The effect can actually be the opposite, one of cocooning. The use of stone in dark colors creates the same effect. Dark gray slates are beautiful, although costly. Black marble offers a feel of luxury and presence; it can be also used in smaller doses in a kitchen or bathroom as a backsplash or countertop.

The range of midtone grays in Night Shadows, like ash and gunmetal, are versatile and unassuming. They invite us to look beneath the surface and explore the quality of the material in a space. In these colors, natural fibers, interesting weaves, and embossed materials will all stand out, as will the detail on the texture of stone or wood, so make sure to choose well-constructed materials of the best quality to evoke understated luxury.

Today near eventime I did lead
the girl who has no seeing
a little way into the forest
where it was darkness and shadows were.
I led her toward a shadow
that was coming our way.
It did touch her cheeks
with its velvety fingers.
And now she too
does have likings for shadows.
And her fear that was is gone.

—OPAL WHITELEY, "The Story of Opal," 1920

5

Whisper

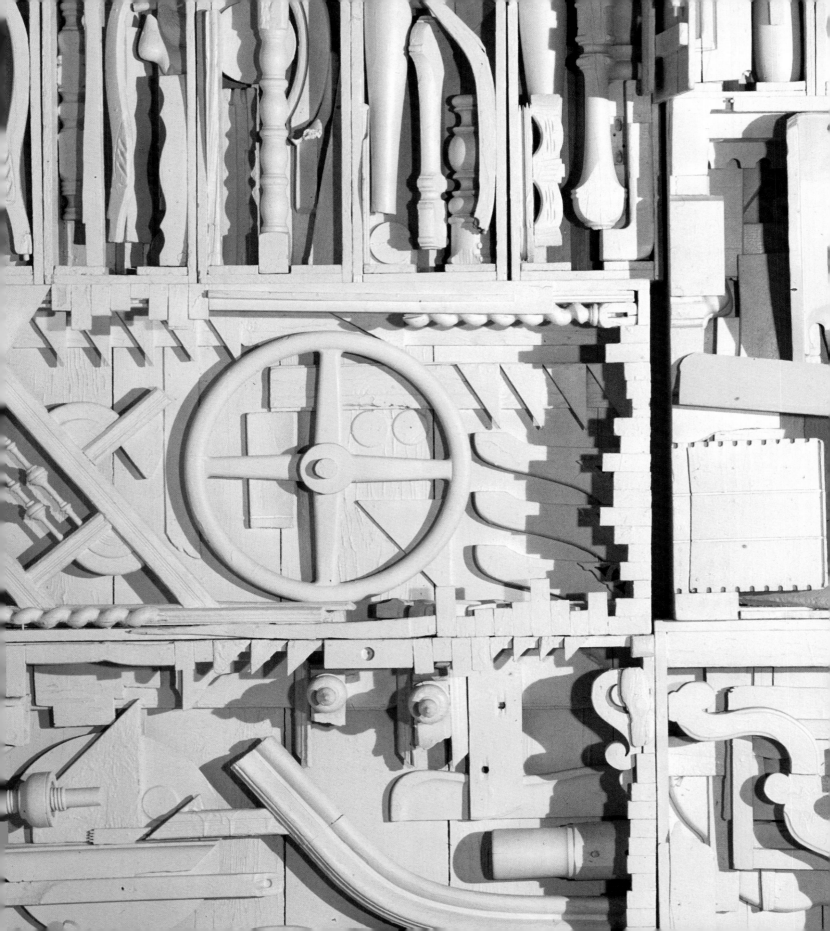

Quietude

St. Peter's Lutheran Church, a modern stone-and-glass building on the corner of Lexington Avenue and Fifty-fourth Street in Manhattan, is situated in one of the busiest, and noisiest, areas of the city; its mission is to serve "life at the intersection." It is an unlikely location for an oasis of calm, but there is one in the late sculptor Louise Nevelson's stunning permanent installation, which composes the church's Chapel of the Good Shepherd. A five-sided room measuring twenty-one by twenty-eight feet, it is, as the church describes it, a "comprehensive sculptural environment," in which visitors are surrounded by large wooden sculptures attached to the walls, all painted white, save the white-and-gold cross.

Immerse yourself in Nevelson's sculptural space, and you'll learn what white and its close relatives can do. Illumination from the ceiling and frosted glass on one end of the room plays off the walls and sculptures, casting pale hues of blue, gold, and sometimes pink. The sculptures cast shadows, which move gently with changes in light, or the viewer's location. There is an opalescence to the artist's sculptures, and the pale casts of color in the room keep it from being anesthetizing. The space is tranquil and cleansing, yet it is not barren or sterile.

I have come to call the extraordinarily subtle casts of hue that I saw in the chapel "Whisper colors." Like Nevelson's sculptures, Whisper colors live in an intersection between committed color and white. They are there, but barely. They have an impact on us, but it is a gentle one. You can see them in sea foam, corn silk, and water chestnuts as well as alabaster and other seashells.

Whisper colors demand nothing of us. They are not a call to action or an aid to focusing our energies or moods on specific goals. They make space for us to think, to breathe in, to quiet ourselves, to rest.

Dove

Blush

Calm

Celestial

Whitewash

Still

Soft

Nuanced

Ash

Delicate

Seraphic

Vanilla

Patient

Opaline

Diaphanous

Composed

Ice pink

Pearl

Nude

Alabaster

Spiritual

Harmonious

Bone

Oyster

Bisque

Subtle

Airy

Ivory

Jasmine

Porcelain

Nacre

"At the symbolic level, silence is a part of every sacred tradition, for each knows that profound mysteries may address us only in silence."

—AMI RONNBERG, *The Book of Symbols*, 2010

All About White

Anyone who has been tasked with selecting a white paint color has glimpsed the vastness of the white world and the confusion that can reign there. Alter any one of white's constituent colors and you alter white, coaxing out an undertone or casting a pale hue. Some major paint manufacturers offer 150 or more shades of white, with inventive names designed to capture their subtleties; references to the Arctic, snow, or water may tell us they are cooler whites with blue or black undertones, while references to hot beverages or desert sands almost always steer us to the warmer ones. But where white ends and other colors begin in the retail paint world is hard to discern. Valspar's 167 whites include Fainting Violet and Orchid Ash, while Benjamin Moore's 157 feature Summer Peach and Celery Salt.

The most important consideration in selecting the perfect white is the intensity of light in the space in which you will use it. Cool whites are better suited to sunny spaces, while warmer whites are best suited to spaces with less light. Titanium white and bone white are good examples of cool whites, and there are many variations on these colors available from paint retailers. Ivory and cream are warm whites, and they too are available in abundance.

Do not try to pick one white for your entire home. Rarely is light evenly distributed throughout every room, so the same paint will have different effects in different rooms. It requires effort to customize your whites in this way, but the final result will be far more pleasing.

Regardless of the whites you choose, you can always count on them to create an expanded sense of space and to provide the cleanest backdrop for artwork and furnishings. We may think of white as a "safe" bet, but that is because it is a reliable asset in almost all interiors.

Softly, Now

The pearl is the first gem known to humankind, and while most jewelry is fashioned from metals or gemstones derived from the earth, the pearl is the only one to be produced by a living creature. Ancient cultures and religions worldwide endowed pearls with mystical significance, using them as symbols of value, purity, perfection, and the divine. In Hinduism the pearl is associated with the god Krishna, who is said to have plucked the first pearl from the sea as a gift to his daughter on her wedding day. Ancient depictions of Persian queens show them wearing pearl pendant earrings, a sign of their status. The Chinese used the pearl as a symbol of the Tao, while in the New Testament pearls represent whatever is most precious, including the kingdom of heaven with its pearly gates. Unimpeded by advances in science, intellectuals and poets throughout the ages attributed the pearl's subdued luster to its origin in fairy tears, angel tears, or dew drops, its subtle iridescence an echo of its watery provenance.

The worth ascribed to these bewitching gems among diverse people and at different stages of history is the stuff of legend. Before cultivated pearls became available in the twentieth century, only the very rich and royal could afford them. According to the ancient historian Pliny the Elder, Cleopatra won a bet with Marc Antony that she could spend a literal fortune—ten million sesterces—on a single meal, which she accomplished by dissolving a pearl in vinegar and drinking it. Elizabeth I famously wore pearls from head to toe, appropriate raiment for a Virgin Queen, but the sumptuary laws of the time strictly limited the wearing of pearls by her subjects in order to avoid confusion among the classes—as well as to discourage the ruinous expenditure necessary to acquire them. Pearls were still an extravagant expense in 1917, when Jacques Cartier acquired the lot at 653 Fifth Avenue in Manhattan, where the famed jeweler's flagship store still stands. The price? According to Hans Nadelhoffer in his book, *Cartier: Jewelers Extraordinary*, it was a double-strand pearl necklace valued at $1 million, or about $18 million in today's dollars.

By turns demure and sensuous, pearls retain their air of understated opulence, even in our more-is-better world. Sometimes, there is just no need to shout.

"I was the Angel, who of old bowed down
From heaven to earth and shed that tear, O Pearl
From which thou wert first fashioned in thy shell."

—FRIEDRICH RUCKERT, "Edelstein und Perle," *Gedichte von Friedrich Rückert,* 1847

"Heard melodies are sweet; but those unheard are sweeter."

—JOHN KEATS, "Ode on a Grecian Urn," 1820

Just sit there right now
Don't do a thing
Just rest.

For your separation from God,
From love,

Is the hardest work
In this
World.

Let me bring you trays of food
And something
That you like to
Drink.

You can use my soft words
As a cushion
For your
Head.

—HAFIZ, "Just Sit There Right Now," *Love Poems from God*, c. fourteenth century

Layering with Whisper

There is no palette more conducive to layering than Whisper colors. Vanilla, cream, oyster, parchment, opaline-light celadon, and ice pink all layer beautifully. The colors may be subtle (think of them as halftones), but when displayed in varying textures and shades, they make an impact through interest and innuendo, rather than through a bold statement.

The best rooms for layering Whisper colors are living rooms and bedrooms, those spaces in which we seek calm and serenity and a degree of quiet. They are not ideal for rooms reserved for activity (like family rooms or playrooms) or where a great deal of energy is required.

The optimal way to use Whisper colors is to combine many soft and nuanced tones in a single space or area. Walls and floors that are stripped down to their original state or are whitewashed will bring texture to the foreground. Light-colored marble is a great stone to use because of its cloudy translucency, although I'd recommend using it as an accent to maintain its subtlety. Sliding white shoji screens and handmade paper panels between glass dividers will help to define spaces that are decorated in Whisper colors by providing necessary grounding for this ethereal palette.

Texture is critical to showing off the palette to its best advantage. The more subtle the colors, the more texture is needed to create interest and dimension in a space. Combine textiles such as chenille, velvet, dupioni silk, and taffeta silk with marble, wood, and ceramic finishes in the same room, as the juxtapositions between these materials will make the look come alive.

Vary the light opacity in the fabrics you choose for the windows. A sheer transparent layer of drapes allows light in, but also provides privacy. If you add a second track of opaque drapes in a light color, the combination will give you greater control over the light in the space, and the layers create a dimensional appearance. Remember that, in general, this palette likes brighter light, which shows off its subtleties at its finest.

You can add a bit of luster or pearlescense to reflect light and accessorize in the same palette. This is best done with objects like vases and trays (think mother-of-pearl), artwork, or collections of seashells that sit on side tables or windowsills.

"Have you ever heard
the wonderful silence
just before the dawn?
Or the quiet and calm
just as a storm ends?
Or perhaps you know
the silence when you
haven't the answer to
a question you've been
asked, or the hush of a
country road at night, or
the expectant pause of a
room full of people when
someone is just about to
speak, or, most beautiful
of all, the moment
after the door closes
and you're alone in the
whole house? Each one is
different, you know, and
all very beautiful if you
listen carefully."

—NORTON JUSTER
The Phantom Tollbooth, 1961

If These Walls
Could Talk (Softly)

Because of their subtlety, Whisper colors are ideal for wallcoverings
that add interest as a backdrop without distracting from the
artwork displayed on them. I once designed one such wallcovering,
"stringing" strands of chenille yarn in the warp direction and
anchoring them to a paper ground; I like to refer to it as "velvet
for the wall." I have done the same with a dressier silk yarn, as
well as a more casual bouclé yarn. Using these types of texturized
wallcoverings in oyster, buff, and champagne tones adds dimension
to a room as well as a sense of luxe and sophistication without
limiting other decorating options.

Lullaby

Lullabies are as old as human existence, and some ancient music experts believe that we are simply wired for them. The British Museum in London, for example, houses a four-thousand-year-old small clay tablet, Babylonian in origin, inscribed with the words to a cradle song. Numerous studies have demonstrated the beneficial effects of lullabies—and other forms of soothing music and rhythms—on babies, particularly ailing ones. They lower heart rate, increase alertness during waking hours, and aid sleep.

Recent studies suggest that adults can benefit from lullabies too. Music, which is composed of vibrations or sound waves of varying lengths, alters our brain waves and

heartbeats in measurable and predictable ways through a process called *entrainment*. Exposure to classical and meditative music in particular has been shown to relieve stress, reduce pain, enhance the immune system, and increase mental clarity, even in the face of neurological illness.

There are benefits for the lullaby singer as well. Singing, even humming, are stress relievers that have been found to increase feelings of well-being. But lullabies, which have sad or even frightening lyrics as well as happy ones (the Babylonian example in the British Museum scolds a baby for waking the house god with its crying), also give singers a chance to unburden without fear of censure or embarrassment. Expressing our emotions in dulcet tones and hypnotic rhythms—be they feelings of love or worry—can help us find peace.

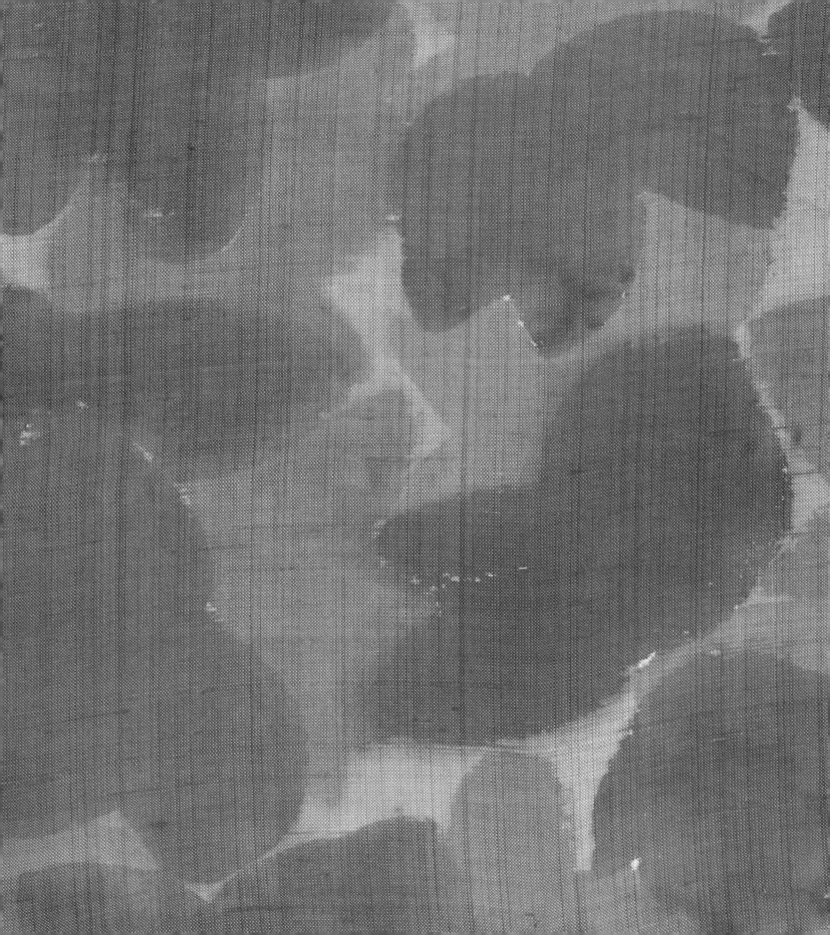

6

Earthly

"Beauty is an ecstasy; it
is as simple as hunger."

—W. SOMERSET MAUGHAM, *Cakes and Ale*, 1930

Elementary

I had been doing business with textile mills in India for years before I had the opportunity to visit. Everything about the country and its people struck me as exotic and dramatic. I bought every photography book on India I could find, as the images I saw there— the food markets, clothing, buildings, and landscapes—all radiated with colors I found rapturously beautiful—sienna, madder, terra-cotta, purple, burnt umber. When I finally arrived there, I had grand plans for exploring the place on my own. I wanted to walk the streets and touch the wares and see the sights, much as I had done during my travels in Europe and the United States.

That did not happen. As my business colleagues there had predicted, I was overwhelmed the moment I left my hotel in Delhi. There were throngs of people—begging, offering tours, hoping to sell me trinkets or crafts. The intense heat of the day covered me like a heavy wool blanket, leaving me wet with perspiration and dry mouthed. The smell of so many diverse spices, at once strange and familiar—cumin, rasam, coriander, and sambar— was almost as disorienting as the din of bicycle bells, shouting merchants, and Indian music. So I retreated and did what so many foreigners do: I hired a guide and saw the country mostly from behind the glass of a car window.

I saw poverty the likes of which I had never seen before: families living in cardboard boxes, children wandering the roads unattended, animals in the street. Yet I also saw what I can only describe as an irrepressible drive to possess, make, and live surrounded by beauty. In Bangalore, my next stop, flowers were abundant and explosively colorful—jacaranda, gulmohur, raintree, and copper pod—and the locals cut them, wore them, and peddled them. I saw destitute women and men creating gorgeous materials and useful objects in which they took unmistakable pride, and I saw young children playing happily, making use of the most humble objects—natural and man-made—to fuel their games and imaginations.

The people, even in the poorest areas, were stunning; they carried themselves with dignity and adorned themselves with the most attractive things they could find. Through the red dust kicked up from the unpaved roads, the women's saris were vibrant, even breathtaking, in shades of red, magenta, and gold, among others.

In India I learned never to underestimate the power of beauty—the universal thirst for it, its elemental role in bringing joy to our passage through life. Beauty enlivens and satisfies us. It intensifies our experiences, humbles us, and exalts us and the world around us. None of us is ever too small, too poor, or too lost to partake in it.

Amethyst

Cayenne

Exotic

Terra-cotta

Sexual

Passionate

Burnt sienna

Resourceful

Unconventional

Clay

Auburn

Adobe

Expressive

Temperamental

Artistic

Brick

Individual

Dramatic

Cinnamon

Ochre

Rust

Cochineal

Caramel

Assertive

Powerful

Chutney

Aubergine

Fierce

Ardent

Living with Earthly

The lovely baked hues of the Earthly color world are comfortable and inviting, recalling the natural beauty of the cavernous colored canyon rock throughout the American West and the rolling landscapes of Tuscany. Decorating with these colors—ochre, burnt orange, cinnabar, and umber—can bring the same warmth into your home.

The most dramatic way to integrate these colors into a home is to use materials in which the color is naturally present. A wall or two of exposed red clay brick in a family room or kitchen adds a timeless warmth to these spaces that works with any furnishing style. Brick can create a rustic look, to be sure, but it is equally at home in urban industrial-style lofts or antique-filled rooms. If the prospect of exposed brick seems overwhelming or too expensive, terra-cotta tiles offer a similar warmth in a more understated way. Like brick, terra-cotta tiles are versatile; in addition to flooring, they are beautiful in backsplashes and can be displayed as decorative wall pieces. For larger wall areas, consider the ancient Moroccan plasterwork technique called *tadelakt*, in which a limestone plaster is covered in soap and buffed or rubbed with a stone to create a beautiful, polished surface that is water-resistant and durable. Mixed with clay, it yields authentic earthly colors in a variety of hues.

Earthly colors are adept at creating a cozy, intimate, and contained atmosphere. Sienna velvet upholstery, cochineal-colored fabric, burnt-orange chenille throws, and sorrel accessories are just some of the ways this palette can create that sense of intimacy. Candle and firelight enhance them, so choose them for rooms that you use in the evening and let them warm you.

Henna

A Hindu woman traditionally decorates herself with henna, a practice known as Mehndi, on the occasion of her wedding, an act rich in symbolism, for it is believed to connect her to Lakshmi, the goddess of prosperity, who dwells in henna designs. It is also thought to protect her from misadventure and make her more alluring, a belief with roots in the Hindu myth of Parvati, who was able to appease and charm the powerful Lord Shiva by decorating herself with henna.

To prepare for Mehndi, dried henna leaves are ground into a fine powder and combined with water to create a paste. Other ingredients may be added to intensify its color, such as cardamom, dried pomegranates, tamarind, or tea water. After the paste has set over the course of a few hours, it is placed in a cone-shaped dispenser from which it is squeezed in a thin line onto the skin of the bride. Designs may be inspired by ancient symbols or motifs—such as lotus flowers, which connote the awakening of the soul, or *satkonas*, six-pointed stars that represent the union of male and female—but creativity and originality are also valued in the art of Mehndi, leaving room for unique configurations.

Mehndi is not the sole preserve of brides. The art is practiced during festive occasions and celebrations as a symbol of joy, luck, and prosperity and is passed down through oral tradition.

Wonder

When my daughter Emma was nine, we came across some pomegranates at the market. I have always thought pomegranates were a beautiful fruit—elegant, intensely earthy, the composition and content of their interiors surprising. I wanted my daughter to experience them, so we purchased one, and when we got home, I cut into the fruit to reveal the intricate, vibrant beauty of its numerous seeds. The ruby juice ran onto the counter, where I, uncharacteristically, let it stand so that she could admire it.

Emma examined the fruit. "Mommy," she asked, "who designed this? It is really pretty."

Wonder comes effortlessly to the young. They may marvel at the interesting construction of a common kitchen pan or the way the stem of a leaf is connected to the tiny veins that feed it, while adults look upon those same objects as things to be washed or raked. We know when something pleases us, but we seldom stop long enough to examine what it is about its appearance, sound, taste, smell, or touch that makes it so pleasing.

I am often asked where I find the inspiration for my designs. My answer is simple: everywhere. But if I am pressed to provide specifics, I might mention nature, tea, music, scents, art, fashion, emotions, artifacts, children, my children, snow, sun, history, autumn. There is so much to inspire us if we could just slow down long enough to pause, to take in and hold on to the varied experiences our five senses bring.

Saffron

Saffron announces itself only in the golden yellow tips of the red stigmas inside a delicate purple flower. It takes a color of such exceeding beauty and a spice of such rich earthiness to warrant the painstaking process of harvesting these stigmas—three per flower, picked by hand, at dawn—from the *Crocus sativus*, or saffron crocus—which blooms only once before dying. Between two hundred thousand and four hundred thousand of these carefully dried stigmas are required to make two pounds of saffron. The most expensive spice in the world, saffron has been used over the centuries as a food coloring, a hair and nail dye, a fragrance, and as a substitute for gold leaf in illuminated manuscripts. Perhaps most famously, saffron is the color of choice for the robes of Buddhist monks, although the spice is too costly for such a purpose today; monks now color their robes with saffron substitutes, such as synthetic dyes or turmeric. Saffron produces an unstable pigment, the intensity of its dye diminishing from a luminous orange gold to paler shades of yellow with wash, wear, and sun exposure.

Earthly Purple

You can enhance the browns, rusts, and pomegranates of the Earthly palette with touches of a lesser-used member of the palette: purple. Traditionally associated with royalty, purple adds luxury to a color world that can feel unpolished. Try combining purple with golden hues—like ochre and mustard—in a supporting role: the backs of dining room chairs, in passementerie, and in artwork. In a den or family room, this color combination works beautifully on throws or on lampshades for added drama.

I love a sunburnt country,
A land of sweeping plains,
Of ragged mountain ranges,
Of droughts and flooding rains.
I love her far horizons,
I love her jewel-sea,
Her beauty and her terror—
The wide brown land for me!

—DOROTHEA MACKELLAR, "My Country,"
My Country and Other Poems, 1909

Awakening

Many years ago, when I was single and fresh out of college, I visited friends at their rented home on Cape Cod. I was one of a handful of visitors, which included a handsome stranger who, like me, suffered from insomnia. While our hosts slept, he would read aloud to me from a novel, almost certainly one set at the turn of the twentieth century. I wish I could remember the title of the book, but I can't. I recall only that its characters discovered in themselves, and struggled to contain, emotions and passions that they had been taught were unacceptable, even unseemly. Despite the understated style of the prose, it was heady stuff for a very young woman on her own for the first time. What was so captivating was the characters' inability to keep their desires repressed—and that this was revealed to me by an appealing fellow in the middle of the night in a house by the sea.

It wasn't until some years later, when I watched Merchant Ivory's adaptation of Forster's *A Room with a View*, that I experienced this theme in all its fullness. Of course, the romance at the center of the story is satisfying: Lucy, a young, well-heeled British woman visits Italy, where she embarks on a journey of self-discovery that carries her across class lines to marry the man she really loves despite the disapproval of her family and friends. But what resonates so strongly is not the love story per se, but the force of the passions that overturn our heroine's well-ordered world, passions that are stronger and larger than anything her Edwardian upbringing has prepared her for: forbidden desire, violence and death, the blunt force of prejudice, the beauty of nature, the beauty of art—the fire of life. She must decide whether to retreat to safety or advance into the fire. She advances.

We never get to see the life that Lucy goes on to lead once she marries. Whether it was unconventional or dull, it doesn't matter. The point is that she was fully awake when she chose it.

"Live in each season as it passes; breathe the air, drink the drink, taste the fruit, and resign yourself to the influence of the earth."

—HENRY DAVID THOREAU, *Walden*, 1854

7

At Ease

P-33   Arizona Biltmore, Phoenix, Arizona

6A-H705

Oasis

When the Arizona Biltmore opened in an isolated section of the Sonoran Desert outside Phoenix in 1929, the area was not a popular vacation destination; nonetheless, thehotel was an instant sensation, quickly becoming known as "the Jewel of the Desert." Celebrities frequented the Arizona Biltmore from its earliest days, lending the hotel an enduring glamour. Marilyn Monroe favored its Catalina Pool. Clark Gable played golf there, temporarily losing his wedding ring on the course. Irving Berlin wrote "White Christmas" during a visit, reportedly poolside. Presidents Harry S. Truman and John F. Kennedy stayed at the resort, among other U.S. presidents, and Tony Bennett, Bing Crosby, and Liza Minnelli were all spotted there.

The Arizona Biltmore's greatest claim to fame is its status as an architectural masterpiece that achieves beauty and an effortless elegance with simple materials and invitees an interior design reflecting the color palette of the desert. Albert McArthur, with input—the amount of which has been debated for decades—from his former teacher, Frank Lloyd Wright, built the hotel with sand from the desert around it, casting it on-site into 250,000 concrete textile blocks imprinted with art deco motifs inspired by the trunk of the palm tree. These "Biltmore Blocks" were also installed in the walls of the hotel lobby, interspersed with semi-opaque glass fixtures of the same dimensions. Shortly after the hotel opened, the *Arizona Republic* observed that their effect "removes the curse of barrenness clinging to all previous attempts at modern architecture." The blocks are remarkable for the manner in which they allow the sun to illuminate and warm the hotel over the course of the day, casting lighter and darker shades of dove, ash, ecru, and fawn, against which the usually blue sky shows in brilliant relief.

The resort's design and neutral palette was, and still is, at once glorious and unobtrusive. It is a spectacular example of what the At Ease palette can do: allow us to relax.

Casual   Kind

Dependable

Sand   Honest   Flexible

Easygoing   Beige

Raffia   Walnut   Open-minded

Accessible   Biscuit

Natural   Linen

Acorn

Oatmeal

Friendly   Tea   Straightforward

Wheat   Courteous

Carefree   Content   Tan

Mocha   Taupe

Khaki   Straw

Ecru   Café au lait

The Allure of Neutrals

In my textile and wallcovering business, the best-selling colors, regardless of pattern, texture, or application, are always neutrals. Whether they are warm or cool, light or midtone, neutrals are the most popular colors among my clients.

There is no color group that imparts greater ease to its users, both in terms of its effect and its versatility, for neutrals can be the star or the supporting cast in an interior. A room can feature a wholly neutral palette—an approach that is at once sophisticated and casual—or it can use neutrals as the backdrop for other color selections to endless effect, particularly if the items of color are accessories such as pillows, a casual throw, and decorative ceramics.

The rooms in this second category are the chameleons; if you remove the statement colors and replace them with new ones, the room is transformed. This technique works in virtually any room in the home, but it adds a degree of comfort and ease to living and entertaining spaces in particular that other styles cannot rival. To jazz up a neutral palette, add classic jewel tones like emerald, burgundy, or royal blue, or add a multicolor suzani throw or a patterned Oriental rug.

All-neutral rooms are elegant in their understatement and an excellent way to accentuate the texture of fabric. The quieter the neutral, the more pronounced the texture will be, so choose light neutral fabrics with weaves that add interest. One benefit of decorating in neutrals is that you cannot make a mistake with them. Go with whatever tones you love—beiges, taupes, ecrus, sandstones—and sink into them.

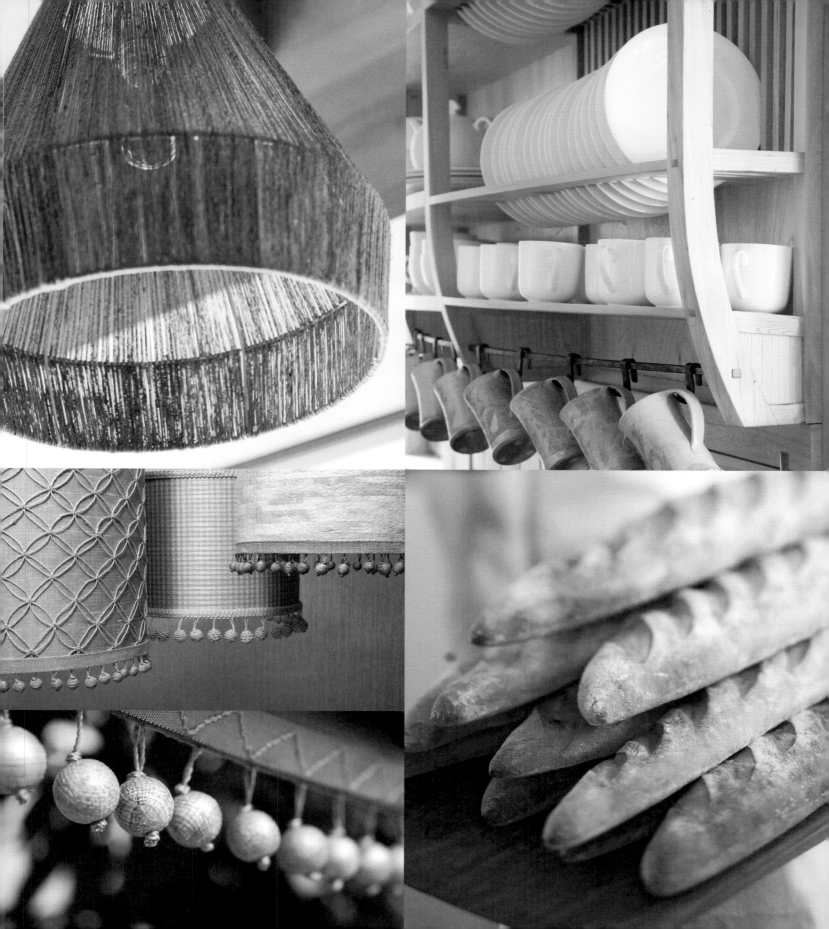

World on a String

In early 2015, at age seventy-three, Bob Dylan released *Shadows in the Night*, an album of American standards composed of songs that Frank Sinatra recorded in the 1940s, 1950s, and 1960s. The unexpected combination of Dylan's gravelly voice and the mellow rhythms of the ballads piqued the interest and admiration of critics. Dylan's was only the most recent in a long line of albums by contemporary artists that have successfully revisited the songs of great twentieth-century American composers and reinterpreted the recordings of famous crooners. From Linda Ronstadt, who recorded three albums with the Nelson Riddle Orchestra, to Tony Bennett and Lady Gaga teaming up on their record *Cheek to Cheek*, and from Harry Connick Jr. and Michael Bublé to Michael Feinstein, who have all made a career of performing standards and original pieces that sound old-school, their music recalls the mellow romanticism of the crooner era.

Seductive, soothing crooning may seem old-fashioned, but it's actually a by-product of the twentieth-century invention of the microphone. Before Rudy Vallee and Bing Crosby purred and trilled into microphones in the late 1920s and 1930s, belters, like Al Jolson, were prized for their ability to project their voices to the far reaches of performance halls. With amplification, singers could deliver the mellow, relaxed, more natural performances now associated with legends like Frank Sinatra, Dean Martin, Mel Tormé, and Sammy Davis Jr.

Crooning evokes more than a bygone era; it evokes the sense of leisure, relaxation, and glamour embodied in the iconic venues where Sinatra and company entertained audiences

looking to unwind—posh supper clubs serving food and cocktails, such as the La Ronde Supper Club in Miami Beach's Fontainebleau Hotel or the Copa Room at the now-defunct Sands Hotel and Casino in Las Vegas. Stylishly cool and nonchalant, unapologetically inspiring indulgence, these crooners invited their fans to lean back and go for the ride, even if just for the duration of a song and a cocktail.

Bringing Nature In

Infusing your home with decorative touches from nature creates visual interest and a relaxed atmosphere. A collection of smooth egg-shaped stones in a wood bowl, shells and sand—combined or alone—in hurricane lamps or glass votives create a timeless look that enhances every kind of decor. I have a friend who collects sand from every beach she visits. She displays her collection in decorative glass bottles, each labeled with the beach of origin, giving the arrangement an intriguing museum-like quality. The same could be done with other natural "artifacts," like rocks and pebbles, driftwood, coral, and even sea glass.

Perfectly Imperfect

For many years now I have been privileged to work with a group of artisans in a small village in the Philippines, where much of the paper for my wallcoverings is made entirely by hand in a beautiful open-air facility. By modern manufacturing standards, the work space is primitive—long tables, benches, and vats on a concrete floor—as are the materials we use, which are primarily fibers from plants, leaves, and tree bark that are indigenous to the islands. We use salago and abaca fibers, which are coarse and strong; pina fiber (from the leaves of the pineapple tree), which is somewhat finer; and the longer fibers from the bark of the mulberry tree, which have a distinct softness. We create pulp from the fibers in various combinations and, when we have found the right mix, we craft beautifully patterned paper panels from them.

These panels are not perfect. Their natural colors vary over a sizable range of neutrals, from cream to parchment to straw to wheat. There are irregularities in their textures, which create uneven patterning on their surfaces. No two panels are identical, because they reflect the imperfections inherent in handcrafting and the vagaries of nature. Sometimes we dye them, and I have gilded some too. But their natural, neutral colors, which highlight the irregularities in the paper, are the ones that attract the most attention. They exude an ease that tempers formality and relaxes the spaces they grace. Their casual colors and tropical fibers have furnished private homes and fancy hotels, even a few department stores in bustling cities, and in all these places, their wonderful imperfections—that human touch— provide relief from the hard edges and straight lines that surround them.

Caramel-Coated Popcorn, Peanuts, and a Prize

German immigrants Frederick and Louis Rueckheim of F.W. Rueckheim & Brother had been making and selling popcorn in the Chicago area for twenty years when in 1893 they hit upon a variation that would become a behemoth among snack foods: popcorn and roasted peanuts coated in a light golden layer of molasses. Legend has it that the brothers happened upon the name a few years later, after a salesman sampled the concoction and declared, "That's crackerjack!"—slang for "first-rate." The Rueckheims trademarked the Cracker Jack name in 1896, the same year that Louis refined the molasses coating to prevent the popcorn from sticking together, thus putting the finishing touch on a recipe that has been enjoyed for more than a century in fifty countries around the world.

But it took more than a good recipe and a catchy name to turn the Rueckheims' invention into the feel-good snack tradition it is today. It took fun. In 1908, Jack Norworth immortalized the brand, and its association with baseball—"America's pastime"—in the lyrics to his wildly popular ballad, "Take Me Out to the Ball Game." The Rueckheims built on this public relations windfall in 1912, when they decided to include a prize in every package of Cracker Jack—a whistle, a puzzle, toy jewelry, or a baseball card—a master stroke that catapulted the confection to immense popularity and secured it as the stuff of happy childhood memories.

By 2012, Cracker Jack had given away twenty-three billion such treasures buried within its layers of crunchy caramel corn and peanuts. Despite enormous competition in the snack food industry, and scores of rival caramel corn brands, Cracker Jack remains a staple in concession stands at virtually every baseball stadium in the United States. Children and adults still munch their way to the prizes inside, and "Take Me Out to the Ball Game" is still sung at the seventh inning stretch, celebrating Cracker Jack's place among the pleasures of the game.

Best Buddy

As a child, I lobbied my parents, for years and years, to get a dog. I asked for a dog at least once a month. I drew countless pictures of my imagined dog: my dog and I playing; my dog walking; my dog running; my dog licking my face. I still have some of those pictures, because my mother kept a select few as a testament to my desire.

When I was thirteen, my parents finally relented, and our dog, Ginger, arrived just in time to see me through the turbulent waters of adolescence. Every evening, I snuck downstairs and retrieved her from her pen and took her to my room to sleep with me. I returned her before my parents came downstairs each morning.

Ginger, of course, kept our secret and the many others that I could tell no one else. She asked nothing of me but food, water, and a little attention, and she repaid me a hundredfold with her earnest, uncomplicated affections. I don't know if I could draw a picture today that captures the essence of that relationship, but for anyone who has ever anchored themselves in the unconditional love of a dog, I know I don't have to.

Loving Linen

Linen is natural, casual, and livable. I favor linen for slipcovers in simple plain weaves with a slub that gives the fabric an organic, easygoing feel. Keep the colors understated to highlight this texture: gull, parchment, and bisque are all good candidates. When I design using linen, I sometimes add a playful touch—like a floral print— to an organic linen ground, which can be used for drapery or upholstery. This approach works best when the colors of the print are also neutral, like shades of beige and wheat.

Linen's tendency to crease and wrinkle is, to me, one of its greatest qualities; it bears the marks of usage in a way I find interesting and beautiful. If you're bothered by wrinkles, choose a fabric that combines linen with hemp. You will get the same casually elegant look but without as much creasing.

Linen is extremely versatile. You can dress it up or down. Lined, it can be used for drapes that create a polished look. Unlined, it creates a more casual, earthy look. Linen in its purest form is light and summery, but if you want to make it more multiseasonal, choose a linen velvet, which is suitable for all seasons and decor styles. The pile color naturally shifts, giving the fabric some movement and variation. Most muted colors work well for linen velvet, but especially sand, ecru, and taupe.

When using linen in a space, I prefer to use all natural fibers in the other elements of the decor. Silk, wool, cotton, and bamboo are all good candidates for the complementary upholstery and can be accented by stoneware, sisal rugs, natural woods, simple rough-hewn furniture, and other handcrafted materials.

"All in the golden afternoon
Full leisurely we glide ..."

—LEWIS CARROLL, *Alice's Adventures in Wonderland*, 1865

8

Out Loud

Living Out Loud

Sonia Delaunay already was an accomplished painter when, in 1912, she completed the project believed to have put her on the path to becoming one of the greatest abstract artists and colorists of the twentieth century: a patchwork baby blanket for her infant son, featuring blocks of solid-colored fabrics with stitched curves cutting through the otherwise linear motif. The blanket combined traditional quilting techniques from her native Russia with a groundbreaking use of color, one in which colors displayed in bold geometric shapes are freed from representational form and juxtaposed to tease out their inherent rhythm and movement, their most dynamic, vibrating qualities. She and her husband, French artist Robert Delaunay, called this use of color *simultané*, or "simultaneous contrasts," a term that took on new meaning as she fearlessly broke through the conventional boundaries that separated high art from fashion, traditional from modern techniques, the mundane from the sublime. She made color the meaning and the message in all of her many endeavors, challenging us to reimagine and maximize its role in our lives.

Delaunay's remarkable innovations emerged from a deep understanding of the power of color to move us and the determination to unleash it. Diana Vreeland captured the audacity of Delaunay's color aesthetic in her foreword to *Sonia Delaunay: Art into Fashion*, where she wrote, "her colors didn't fool around—they shot straight for the eye. Yellows as cleansing as the Lisbon sun, reds as powerful as Red Square, blues with no regrets, unrepentant purples, infinite blacks." These colors make Delaunay's paintings riveting; her 1913 composition *Electric Prisms*, for example, is an undulating collage of angular shapes and discs in incandescent blues, greens, reds, purples, pinks, and yellows, enhancing and disrupting each other as their shapes collide and compete for attention. It is a beautiful homage to the shock of intensity that electric lights, relatively new at the time, brought to the colors they illuminated. But her genius, and her celebrity, was rooted in her ability to translate these riotous color arrangements onto other surfaces and into other disciplines, infusing them with the fierce energy of abstract art.

Delaunay began this cross-pollination in her family's home in Paris, which she furnished with lampshades, pillows, and other accents covered in her boldly colored textiles. In 1913, she made and wore a *simultané* dress in blocks of pink, orange, blue, and scarlet, appropriately, for a night of tango at the Bal Bullier, a dance hall in Montparnasse that she and Robert frequented twice a week. It was the first of many such dresses she would create, for herself and others, as her reputation for capturing the cutting edge of modernity swept through the fashion world. The same year, she collaborated on a book with French poet Blaise Cendrars, *La Prose du Transsibérien et de la Petite Jehanne de France* ("The Prose of the

Trans-Siberian and of Little Jehanne of France"), in which Delaunay illustrated Cendrars's poem about a train journey with dynamic hand-painted forms that captured the movement and rhythm of the text. Semicircular shapes in brilliant blues, reds, and greens pulsate down the side of the accordion-folded paper alongside the lines of the poem, accented with lighter shades that add to their vibrancy. Meant to be viewed and read simultaneously, the work was a wildly innovative fusion of the visual and literary arts and a milestone in the development of the artist's book.

In 1917, Sergei Diaghilev, founder of the avant-garde Ballets Russes, tapped Delaunay to design the costumes for the company's production of *Cleopâtré*. The costume she devised for the title role, among others, caused a stir: a sensational narrow gold column dress with layered circular forms of purple, green, red, and blue on the bodice and bust, and a sculptural headpiece with an abstract asp. But Delaunay was just getting started. In the years that followed, she applied her color theory to a dizzying array of creations. She designed fabrics for her own designs and for those of others, including the Metz department store and various textile manufacturers. She produced posters, book covers, necklaces, handbags, children's clothing, bathing suits, shoes, drapes, and parasols in diamonds, zigzags, stripes, and circular patterns of teeming colors that leaped and danced off their surfaces. She sold them from home or from her boutiques in Madrid, Paris, Rio de Janeiro, and other centers of urban sophistication, building a brand and generating demand for her forward-looking aesthetic. In 1924, she established her own textile warehouse, L'Atelier Simultané, where she created fabrics and custom clothing in her signature *simultané* patterns for the likes of Gloria Swanson, Paulette Pax, Jean Patou, and an array of artists and socialites.

The color-soaked abstractions in Delaunay's textiles were distinctly well suited to the simple, vertical silhouettes of women's wear in the 1920s. Those silhouettes began to change at the beginning of the 1930s with the addition of structural details and bias draping, at about the time the global depression was shrinking demand for high-end goods. Delaunay gravitated away from fashion at this point, refocusing on her painting and other projects. She continued to apply her *simultané* techniques for the rest of her life—on canvas, in large murals, in fabric designs, and on smaller objects. Beginning in the 1950s, major museums began showing retrospectives of her art. And in 1964, she became the only woman to be exhibited, in her lifetime, at the Louvre. She died in 1979 at the age of ninety-four.

Sonia Delaunay is credited with many legacies: her use of abstract form to showcase the energy and movement of color; her ability to visually capture, if not define, the modern sensibilities of an era; her disregard for the boundary between high art and everyday life, fine art and the applied arts; and her unprecedented synthesis of entrepreneurism and artistic vision. But her greatest legacy and example may just be that she dared all these things, living as boldly as the colors she showed us.

Energetic

Chartreuse

Lemon yellow

Proud

Vibrant

Magenta

Resolute

Uninhibited

Powerful

Fuchsia

Scarlet

Orange

Resilient

Crimson

Vivacious

Poppy

Ambitious

Outspoken

Free

Ultramarine

Cyan

Violet

Intrepid

Bold

Tangerine

Fearless

Emerald

Kelly green

The Crayola Lexicon

The sight and smell of a new box of Crayola crayons—particularly one with a built-in sharpener—with its stadium-like assembly of perfect paraffin tips is a work of art in itself, a rainbow of possibilities and a conjurer of childhood memories. The distinctive smell of crayons is, according to Yale University, the eighteenth most recognizable scent among American adults. Crayola's vocabulary of color terms and references has, over the years, hinted at a far more complex and intense array of color than the primaries could ever convey: from those that suggest days of old—burnt sienna, celestial blue, and English vermilion—to the natural world—goldenrod, orchid, and jungle green—to fruit—melon, plum, vivid tangerine, laser lemon, jazberry jam, and mango tango—even to a colloquial expression—wild blue yonder.

What began as almost holy perfection could not remain. With use, breakage, and inevitable attrition, the skyline inside the box would change; some crayon tops became rounded; some grew shorter and stood in sharp contrast to the one or two never used; the paper wrappers would tear or come off altogether; and gaps appeared in the lineup. If we thrilled to the new crayon smell, we were not as impressed with the smell of the crayon graveyard that eventually replaced the dilapidated Crayola box, that plastic ice cream tub or old shoe box where we collected the strays, the nubs, the damaged. Yes, we suffered for our art.

In 2008, Crayola marked the fiftieth anniversary of its box of sixty-four crayons by inviting children to propose new names for eight existing crayon colors. Among the winning names were Giving Tree (green), Fun in the Sun (orange), Best Friends (purple), Happy Ever After (blue), and Super Happy (yellow). And today, you can even create a personalized box of sixty-four from the Crayola palette.

Brave New World

The Technicolor Corporation had been struggling to get a toehold in Hollywood for nearly twenty years, until the 1930s, when the company's founder and president, Herbert Kalmus, met with Walt Disney to demonstrate his new process for adding color to film. Technicolor's earlier products had created technical problems with movie projectors that left many studios uninterested in the alleged improvements. The Great Depression, along with Hollywood's entrenched belief that "real" movies were filmed in black-and-white, created additional headwinds for Technicolor. But Kalmus believed that his product was capable of generating vivid, saturated color that could transport a Depression-weary audience from its everyday worries to a more pleasurable world in a way that black-and-white film could not, and he would persist in promoting his vision as long as his very patient investors would allow.

Walt Disney liked what he saw, though, and, despite his brother Roy's objections, forged a relationship with Technicolor in 1932. Walt had big plans too, both for his company and Technicolor: he wanted to make the first ever full-length animated feature film and began production in 1935. Hollywood scoffed at the idea that adults would pay to watch a ninety-minute cartoon and dubbed the project "Disney's Folly." Walt's wife, Lillian, and Roy objected strenuously to the film's staggering $500,000 budget and the riskiness of the venture. When the cost ballooned to an unfathomable $1.5 million, Walt obtained a mortgage on his family's home, and Disney Studios managed to get an additional loan from Bank of America to complete the project.

On December 21, 1937, *Snow White and the Seven Dwarfs* premiered before a sold-out audience—including major stars such as Marlene Dietrich, Charlie Chaplin, Cary Grant, and Shirley Temple—at the Carthay Circle Theatre in Los Angeles. The film changed cinema forever, immersing its viewers in breathtakingly rich color—the finest display of Technicolor to date, according to the critics—and a symphony of music, dialogue, and superb animation that no one had ever seen before or imagined possible. Disney was gratified by the standing ovation *Snow White* received from the naysayers who had ridiculed him, but the $8 million it grossed in the coming months—the most money generated by any movie in the history of film at the time—was the ultimate testament to the grit and courageous determination of Kalmus's and Disney's Technicolor dreams.

Going Bold

Bright colors are energizing. For this reason, places of work and play are better suited to brights than spaces where we relax or sleep.

To my mind, there are two approaches to using these highly saturated colors. The first is as an accent. This is a perfect option for those who want to infuse energy into their interiors in small doses. The Out Loud palette is well suited to entryways or hallways, small spaces that can often use an infusion of bright color. Paint the stair railing in a bold magenta or cobalt, or create a collage of bright primary-colored pictures going up the stairwell. A bathroom is another opportunity to be daring without taking a big risk. Bright blues are perfect in these spaces: I once painted a small bathroom in ultramarine and filled the walls with Matisse prints, creating a pocket of interest and energy in my otherwise very neutral-toned home. In living rooms or family rooms, use bright colors with light to midtone neutrals or bright white to optimize their effect. Throw pillows, rugs, or even a side chair in colors such as cardinal, lime or acid green, fuchsia or bright purple will freshen and contemporize the space. And of course accent walls in any of these colors create a focal point—for activities, artwork, even socializing—without feeling overwhelming.

The second approach to the use of bold colors is to deploy them as the dominant design element in a room or home. The key is to select one or two bright colors of equal intensity and emphasize those colors, with additional brights as accents. A good rule of thumb is to use those major colors in no less than 70 percent of your decorative furnishings and to reserve the other 30 percent of bright colors for accents, preferably in accessories like blankets and pillows, book bindings, pottery, and artwork. Daring red, sunshine yellow, lime green, and cyan are all popular choices for the major notes.

Walls, large pieces of furniture, area rugs, and tables are ideal vehicles for maximizing the impact of these colors. Furnishings with clean simple lines are better suited to these intense hues than more decorative or fussy silhouettes. And if you choose to include some white as a palette cleanser, select crisp whites, not creamy ones, to avoid muddying the palette. Let the bright colors do their energizing work without the weight of lower-energy hues.

Strut

A symbol of pride and ostentation across cultures, the peacock's train is unrivaled in its natural extravagance. A fully grown train is enormous, ranging from three to four feet and comprising more than 60 percent of the bird's length; bright with intense, iridescent colors; and elaborately marked with shapes and patterns.

The peacock's tail confounded Charles Darwin because it made the bird conspicuous to predators and reduced its speed and agility, thereby directly jeopardizing its survival. But Darwin came to understand that at least one thing trumps personal safety in the peacock's priorities: sex. And in the harem-building world of peacocks, color sells.

Peahens are not unique in their preference for bright-colored males. In many species of birds—and animals—displays of bright color play a central role in the ability of males to attract mates. Some aspects of this ritual are invisible to us; birds both possess and perceive colors—including ultraviolet color—that the human eye cannot detect. What appears to us to be a monochromatic male bird may look to his potential partner like a suitor decked out in ultraviolet finery.

Scientists suspect that the female's preference for colorful males is an adaptive one. Research indicates that vibrant colors connote fine health, good nutrition, and promising genes. Darwin's proposed assumption in those early days was simpler: maybe she just likes beautiful things.

The World of Pucci

While it is tempting to attribute a 1960s influence to Emilio Pucci's brightly colored designs and lightweight stretch fabrics, his fashion sense was in evidence decades before he became the darling of fashionable women of the decade. Pucci's vaunted career as a designer and fashion empire builder began in 1947, when photographer Toni Frissell spotted him in Zermatt, Switzerland, wearing a ski outfit of his own design in a stretchy, fitted fabric. After Diana Vreeland, then editor of *Harper's Bazaar*, published the pictures, Pucci was inundated with requests from American companies hoping to make the outfits. He declined those offers in favor of starting his own business in Florence.

The light, stretchy cotton and silk jerseys that came to be one of Pucci's hallmarks were not in vogue when he established his studio; determined to maximize women's freedom of movement, he developed custom stretch fabrics with textiles experts in Italy. Nor were his brilliant, kaleidoscopic prints a common feature in women's wear when he first showcased them on silk scarves in the 1950s; they were a lavish, original fusion of Mediterranean landscape and the diverse motifs and art that Pucci observed in his world travels, rendered in sometimes-shocking hues and combinations: peacock blue and a light silvery yellow; banana and lavender; sapphire and blackberry.

At the suggestion of Stanley Marcus, cofounder of Neiman Marcus, Pucci began using his patterned fabrics in women's dresses and tops. By the early 1960s, Pucci had emerged as the Jet Set's favorite designer, the "Prince of Prints." His clothing was lightweight and versatile, and his custom stretch fabrics made them wrinkle-resistant, a boon for globetrotting celebrities. His dresses adorned some of the most famous and admired women in the world, including Marilyn Monroe, Katharine Hepburn, Elizabeth Taylor, and Jacqueline Kennedy Onassis.

Today, decades after Emilio Pucci's death, the fashion house he founded still thrives, with designs, colors, and patterns that continually reinterpret the charisma of the iconoclast who inspired them.

Dr. Seuss

In 1925, Theodor Geisel was the editor in chief of Dartmouth College's humor magazine, the *Jack-O-Lantern*, when he was caught drinking gin in his room with nine other students. Prohibition was in effect, and the college forced him to resign from the magazine for his infraction. But Geisel would not be deterred: he hatched a plan for continuing his work incognito, publishing his pieces using his mother's maiden name (as well as his middle one): Seuss. He added the title "Dr." many years later as a nod to his father, who had wanted him to earn a doctorate and at whose insistence Geisel attended the University of Oxford to study English literature for a brief period before dropping out.

The world is all the richer for Geisel's decision to pursue his art, and for his perseverance: his first children's book, *And to Think That I Saw It on Mulberry Street*, was rejected by twenty-seven publishers before finding a home at Vanguard Press. As Dr. Seuss, Geisel wrote forty-four books during his lifetime, became the best-selling children's author in the world, and won numerous prestigious prizes including three Academy Awards, two Emmys, a Peabody Award, and the Pulitzer Prize. Dr. Seuss was as famous for his distinctive artwork and bold colors as he was for his whimsical rhymes and characters. Some of his works, such as *The Cat in the Hat*, emphasized primary colors, while others, like *Oh, The Places You'll Go!*, used wildly expressive, saturated colors and busy patterns to create mood and motion. But his most enduring legacy lies in a body of work that reaches, teaches, and entertains children of all ages without condescension or pedantry. His humorous, preposterous rhymes, color-drenched illustrations, and mischievous characters broke the mold of the traditional school primer, creating worlds that we want to live in and learn from. He taught us that reading can, and should, be fun.

You have brains in your head.

You have feet in your shoes.

You can steer yourself any direction you choose.

You're on your own. And you know what you know.

And YOU are the guy who'll decide where to go.

—DR. SEUSS, *Oh, The Places You'll Go!*, 1990

Now every woman can have nails that look lovelier...<u>longer</u>!

Exclusive cream formula puts longer-lasting beauty at your fingertips...*without constant touch-ups!*

Something wonderful happens to your nails with Revlon Nail Enamel. Suddenly, they're *beauties*—transformed by Revlon's fabulous color flattery. *And without constant touch-ups.*

Revlon's cream formula makes the difference! It *moulds* to your nails, *flexes* with them—for greater chip-resistance. For longer-lasting, lovelier manicures, get Revlon Nail Enamel.

. . . .

Have you tried 'Frosted'? When you're in the mood for glitter at your fingertips, Revlon Frosted Nail Enamel is it!

Cream Nail Enamel   .65*
Frosted Nail Enamel .75*
                      *plus tax

Revlon Nail Enamel in 33 fabulous colors

© 1957, REVLON, INC.

Fashionably Red

Designer Christian Louboutin's shoes are a status symbol among fashion cognoscenti, and part of the appeal is that bright red sole, which is synonymous with the brand. The story goes that he was inspired to put bright red bottoms on his shoes when he saw an assistant in his office applying red nail polish. He applied the polish to the bottom of the prototype he was working on, and it made the shoe color "pop," like the Warhol painting he was trying to emulate.

Red lipstick is as old as civilization itself; both men and women in Mesopotamia colored their lips red with pulverized semiprecious stones. Cleopatra favored the color as well and used crushed insects to get just the right hue. Today, there are more lipsticks manufactured in red than any other color.

In L. Frank Baum's *The Wonderful Wizard of Oz*, the magic shoes Dorothy Gale acquires in Munchkinland are silver. Screenwriter Noel Langley changed the shoe color to red for the film adaptation, probably so that they would stand out more on the yellow brick road, and with the help of Technicolor, they did. Dorothy's ruby slippers, now a symbol of the film itself, have inspired little girls, and big ones, ever since.

Natural redheads comprise only 2 percent of the human population, but redheads have figured prominently in history and in our imaginations. Helen of Troy was said to be a redhead. So were Cleopatra and Botticelli's Venus. Hollywood has fed our fascination with gingers too, from Maureen O'Hara and Ann-Margret to Nicole Kidman and Julianne Moore. Of Rita Hayworth, *Esquire* said that "[b]y the end of her famous striptease in *Gilda*, she had removed only a glove and a necklace. It was all she needed to."

Shake It Up

We carefully plan and decorate our homes and work spaces. Sometimes it takes years to complete these projects. In the process we can lose sight of those aspects of our environment that need to change to fit our requirements, evolving tastes, or moods. Innovation and movement reinvigorate us in important ways and, just as important, give us fresh perspectives. They also can make our lives a little easier and a lot more fun.

Sometimes this change is as simple as moving around items that we have stopped noticing. A vase or piece of sculpture can become invisible, or silent, when it occupies the same place day in and day out; we see it and hear it again when it is displayed differently—the same goes for furniture and rugs. Adding touches of intense color to a room can even place every other color in sharper relief.

One of my greatest design inspirations is the bright magnetic alphabet letters that are commonly used on refrigerators. They are ingenious in the way they invite creativity and self-expression: children and adults fiddle with them constantly to make new words and configurations. I had this in mind when I started work on one of my favorite and my most popular wallcoverings, Magnetism. Magnetism has traditional aspects to it: it has a lovely linen surface that is available in a range of colors, from neutrals to brights. But it is also magnetized, making it an ever-changing backdrop for artwork, notes, photographs, posters, and, yes, those plastic alphabet letters. Children love the endless possibilities it offers, but it is used at least as often by adults who value both its utility and changeability.

Breakthrough

When I was in school studying textile design, I idolized Jack Lenor Larsen. We all did. He was a visionary, able to blend traditional weaving techniques with contemporary design to create distinctive artisanal fabrics. I followed his collections and career throughout my early working years in the United States and Europe and was in awe when the Louvre staged an exhibition of his work in 1981, making him one of only four American artists to have been so honored. Working with Larsen was my dream, not unlike the knight Percival, who sought the Holy Grail from King Amfortas.

It took some audacity on my part to make his acquaintance. After seeing images of his designs next to images of mine in a magazine, I tore out the pages and sent them to him with a note suggesting that we meet in person. It was a thin pretense, but it worked. We met in his offices in Manhattan, where we discussed my work and ideas about textile design. But like Percival, who didn't ask the king about his health to obtain the Grail at that first opportunity, I too did not ask the essential question, which in my case, was whether I could come work for him. Instead, I thanked him for his time and left.

I went on to establish my own design business, acquire loyal clients, control my products, set my artistic compass, and report only to myself, but I was not creating the types of high-end contemporary designs I had always wanted to. Then, whether it was luck or fate, four years after our first meeting, Jack called to offer me the position of design director at his company. I was surprised, elated, and conflicted. Working for him had been a long-held ambition, but the thought of giving up what I had built was just as unimaginable as the thought of declining Jack's offer was unbearable.

"I want what isn't possible," I told a wise friend.

"Don't ask for what you think is possible. Ask for what you want," she answered.

When I met with Jack to discuss the offer, he sat at his pristine white desk, chewing on a piece of silk yarn, a habit of his. I sweated, gestured, and presented my case: to be his design director and to continue to run my own design business. I laid it all out for him in full detail—the working arrangement, the level of commitment, how I would balance the two. When I finished talking, I waited for him to speak. There was a long pause.

Finally, he answered: "That sounds fine, Lori."

* * * * * *

Percival came to learn that had he ventured to ask the king about his ailment, the Grail and crown would have been his, and the king's suffering would have been brought to an end. Percival's reticence had cost him dearly. It would be another four years before he made his way back to the Grail. And the second time around, he spoke up.

9

Alchemy

Gold Eternal

In 1328 B.C., when a twenty-two-pound solid gold funerary mask was placed on King Tutankhamun's mummified face and then sealed along with his corpse in a solid-gold coffin, the metal had not yet established itself as the builder of empires or the darling of currencies. It had little role in economic trade at the time; transactions in ancient Egypt were based on the barter system. But already gold had claimed its status as a divine substance suitable for adorning royalty, the better to project a pharaoh's kinship with the golden-skinned deities that Egyptians worshipped, especially the all-powerful sun god Ra. Gold was indestructible and therefore immortal; rare and therefore precious; and above all, it shone with the resplendent beauty of the sun.

Time has not diminished gold's allure. Its distinction as the embellishment of choice in the world's greatest cathedrals, mosques, and palaces has only burnished its reputation over the centuries as the noblest of metals and stoked our obsession with its sumptuous elegance and worth. Gold's combination of beauty and worldly value has made it one of the most coveted substances in history, famous for its outsized role in human affairs and its capacity to tempt, corrupt, and overwhelm human reason. It has launched wars and sustained empires. And it has ruined them too. Indeed, one of the greatest legal battles in art history was waged only recently over Gustav Klimt's magnificent 1907 *Portrait of Adele Bloch-Bauer I*, which came to be known as *The Woman in Gold*.

For the generations of alchemists who strove to turn base metals into it, gold was both an earthly reality and a symbol of spiritual enlightenment; the successful alchemist would be the practitioner who managed to unlock the great mysteries of the natural world and to understand humankind's place in it. Its appeal is eternal; its presence in the everyday, constant. We are moved as much by its historical and symbolic richness as we are by its tangible beauty: as such, its place in language is widespread. It is emblematic of supreme achievement (gold medals), great worth (weight in gold), integrity (gold standard), compassion and purity (heart of gold), supreme goodness (good as gold), divine grace (golden halo), power (crown of gold), achievement and adoration (golden boy or girl), success (striking gold), enduring love (band of gold), prosperity (golden age), longevity (golden years), and the sun's warmth (golden orb).

Ember
Formal
Citrine
Noble
Radiant
Wise
Rose gold
Sunglow
Sumptuous
Honey
Timeless
Exultant
Cognac
Triumphant
Bullion
Beneficent
Alluring
Gold
Magical
Topaz
Elegant
Brass
Amber
Indulgent
Bronze
Copper
Champagne

Gold Accents

In an interior, a small dose of metallic gold goes a long way. Gold frames, accessories like trays, bowls, and vases, and fabrics are regal, beautiful, and rich touches, drawing attention to cherished objects and spaces. Because gold is so evocative, these finishes should be used thoughtfully and with discretion. Other than on walls, where gold leafing can be used beautifully over larger areas, an extravagance of metallic gold can be visually overwhelming and oppressively formal. Metallic gold has a gentler impact when it is combined with soft tones of cream, ecru, sandstone, champagne, and warm white; it's significantly more dramatic when combined with deeper ones, like ruby red, emerald green, and sapphire blue. Gold is definitely at its most dramatic when combined with a deep brown, charcoal, or even black.

Matte gold, in all its forms, has an earthier aura than its metallic counterpart, more burnished in appearance and less yellow, and can be used more liberally without becoming too dressy. Reminiscent of gold that shows signs of age and being handled and well loved over the years, matte gold is a beautiful way to give depth to a room without reflectivity. It is the understated branch of the gold family: impressive without trying too hard, confident without being showy, yet every bit as noble as its flashier cousins that are so highly reflective.

Halcyon Days

The vices and virtues of blond hair have been the subject of some debate ever since the genetic mutation resulting in fair locks took hold in northern Europe some eleven thousand years ago. The Greeks adored golden hair (many gods, as well as Odysseus himself were portrayed as blond), while the Romans initially associated it with prostitutes, who either dyed their hair or wore blond wigs. That changed before Rome fell, again in the Middle Ages, and again during the Renaissance, when fashionable women concocted elaborate systems for exposing their hair to the lightening effects of the sun without darkening their fair skin.

Hollywood has done much to shape our modern sensibilities regarding blondes; sultry Jean Harlow, the original blond bombshell, sparked such a frenzy for her platinum hair color that Howard Hughes offered $10,000 to any colorist who could match the actresses's processed hue. None could. A series of equally iconic blondes followed in her wake—Veronica Lake, Marilyn Monroe, Grace Kelly, Kim Novak, Jayne Mansfield, Brigitte Bardot— inspiring imitators and trends of their own and giving Hollywood glamour a distinctly golden cast that shows no signs of fading, as actresses like Cate Blanchett, Charlize Theron, and Michelle Williams continue to carry the torch.

Gilded Depths

There is gold in ocean water, twenty million tons or so overall, enough to supply every person in the world with nine pounds of it. But the concentration of gold in the earth's waters is so dilute as to be unharvestable; it is measured in parts per trillion.

The ocean floor, though, is a different story. For millennia, seafaring humans have been spilling their treasures into the waters, where they have sunk to unreachable depths. UNESCO estimates that there may be as many as three million shipwrecks beneath the surface of the earth's waters, some number of which are laden with gold and other treasures. Advances in detection and recovery technologies over the last three decades have resulted in a number of such discoveries.

One of the largest treasures recovered to date was discovered in 2007 when an American salvage company located a wreck off the coast of Portugal—which it code-named the "Black Swan"—containing sixteen tons of precious cargo worth an estimated $500 million. Nearly six hundred thousand silver and gold coins were salvaged, along with other artifacts. The Spanish government claimed that the wreck was the *Nuestra Señora de*

las Mercedes, a Spanish frigate sunk by British naval forces in 1804. After hiding the treasure in the United States and battling Spain's legal claims to the haul, the salvagers were ordered in 2012 to surrender it to the Spanish government, which they did via two Spanish military planes.

No one knows for sure how much treasure lies on the ocean floor. Estimates range from tens of billions to hundreds of billions of dollars' worth. Either way, it is enough to inspire treasure hunting for many years to come.

Gold at Home

I call passementerie—tassels, tiebacks, and various other trims—jewelry for the home.
When I design these pieces, they are often inspired by real jewelry, like the collections of
Asprey and Cartier as well as Fabergé's incredible inlay and latticework. In some cases it
is the metal itself I find inspirational. The many shades of gold carats, for example, which
range from 10 (silvery gold) to 24 (yellow gold), show us the variety and richness this
metal has to offer. In measured quantities, all these golds introduce an intense, sophisticated
luster into interiors. But like all jewelry, they must support the overall look of a room, not
overwhelm it.

There are a number of ways to achieve this balance. My favorite use of gold as an
accent is in metal holdbacks or tiebacks for simple solid-colored velvet or silk drapery. The
effect is of a sheath dress showcased with a fabulous decorative belt. It brings interest and
attention to an otherwise basic piece, enhancing both the solid fabric and the gilded accent.
Gold embroidered bullion tape or a fringe of gold metallic yarn to edge drapery or roman
shades is another way to use gold well, as these items add both definition and elegance
to windows. Gold piping lends a discreet luxury to upholstered furniture when used as
welting; it is also dazzling around moldings or along chair rails.

There is a passementerie for every taste and interior style, modern, traditional, rustic.
Find what you love and accessorize.

"No living creature, not even man, has achieved, in the centre of his sphere, what the bee has achieved in her own; and were someone from another world to descend and ask of the earth the most perfect creation of the logic of life, we should needs have to offer the humble comb of honey."

—MAURICE MAETERLINCK, *The Life of the Bee*, 1901

Bees' Gold

Long before scientists were able to map and measure their miraculous lives, bees were an object of human adoration. Their image appears in paintings from the Stone Age, and they are mentioned in some of the earliest writings ever discovered. The Egyptians appreciated the remarkable alchemy that the bees practiced: transforming the warmth of the sun into sweet liquid gold through their indefatigable efforts. It takes twenty-five thousand flights to gather the nectar needed for a pound of honey. The Egyptians believed such inspired work could only come from some divine source, specifically, the tears of Ra, the sun god. As a consequence, bees came to represent immortality and rebirth.

Bees are the only insect to produce a substance that humans consume as food, and honey's warm color, sweetness, and health benefits have endowed it with value through the ages. The ancient Romans paid taxes with honey, as did the Aztecs and Egyptians. It has been used in rituals, as a sweetener, as a wine base, and as a beauty treatment. Its antiseptic and anti-inflammatory properties made it popular for medicinal uses (the Sumerians used it in almost one-third of all prescriptions), many of which continue today.

In its pure state, honey does not spoil. Archaeologists have unearthed many a sealed jar, thousands of years old, yet perfectly preserved and edible. Honey, it turns out, really is eternal.

Thread of Gold

Inspired by the beauty of medieval art, its luminous madonnas and Byzantine splendor, as well as his own love for handcraft, Alexander McQueen's final collection, *Angels and Demons*, was one of the most anticipated of the fall 2010 season in light of the designer's untimely death earlier that year. The collection's allusions to the afterlife evoked emotional responses from some who viewed the collection in Paris, as did its romanticism. The last ensemble to head down the runway was a high-collared cutaway jacket made of gold-lacquered feathers paired with a layered white tulle skirt embroidered delicately with gold at the hem, which the *Wall Street Journal* observed, "created an image of a gold-winged dove flying away."

Beacon of Light

Five years after starting my wallcovering business, I was at a major crossroads. What I was facing was a common dilemma—a creative person starts a business with immeasurable artistic inspiration but without the knowledge and experience needed to operate it—and the pressure to figure out how to get my business on the right track was unrelenting. As a result, my relationships at home and in the office were suffering. I was wilting.

My cousin Stewart, a retired businessman who stood six foot seven and had a commensurately large heart, happened to come to New York at the time and invited me for a drink at the St. Regis Hotel's King Cole Bar. When I got there, I sat down next to Stewart and unburdened myself. I told him about my business and its troubles in detail, and by the time I had finished talking, he had not only diagnosed the problems but also knew how to address them. In an act of generosity that changed the course of my business, Stewart offered his guidance. With a feeling of impossible relief, I accepted.

Stewart became my most cherished mentor and adviser. His gifts to me went well beyond advice concerning business matters. He taught me how to accept constructive criticism, to see the big picture, to make informed decisions, and to be a better listener. He also counseled me to remember that there is always tomorrow; to know what I do best, and to allow others to do what they do best. He saved my business, but more than that, he imparted his wisdom to

me in order that I could save myself. But the greatest lesson Stewart taught me is that we all need someone to light our way every so often. The trick is to be aware of the need, recognize when we are in the presence of one of these guiding lights, and take advantage of the wisdom they have to offer.

Stewart died a few years ago, but he is never far away. I hear him in my head whenever I try to take a shortcut on a business matter or wrestle with the difficulties that all businesses and businesspeople face. I continue to follow his lead and example—and things are working out just fine.

"When all has been said, the adventure of the sun is the great natural drama by which we live, and not to have joy in it and awe of it, not to share in it, is to close a dull door on nature's sustaining and poetic spirit."

—HENRY BESTON, *The Outermost House*, 1928

10

Fragrant Woods

Coming Home

There is a trailhead a quarter mile from the center of Grasmere, a small village in Cumbria, England, which winds its way through the woodlands overlooking the lake for which the village is named and into the noble, ancient colors of Fragrant Woods. The trees that form a canopy over the trail are very old; their massive umber roots protrude from the earth and are gnarled into arresting shapes—natural sculptures centuries in the making. Like almost everything else stationary in these woods—rocks, tree trunks, fence posts—the roots are largely covered in a dense carpet of velvety dark green moss that absorbs sound and light, their sepia bark visible where the moss thins out. The leaves that tower overhead change color with the light, dancing from dusty green and ash to shades of olive and spruce. Brighter green ferns, thigh high and fresh with growth from the frequent rains, inhabit the banks that flank the walking path, a gorgeous complement to the mudstone rocks that form walls along the way and line the path bed. It is only where the trail approaches the edge of the woods, on a steep incline, that the sky's glare and the faraway sounds of human activity intrude. Stepping into the clearing at the end of the path, one can see well into the distance the fells and lakes that receding glaciers left behind millions of years ago and some of the neighboring towns that make up England's Lake District.

The Lake District is renowned for its inviting beauty, but it is the kind of beauty that reminds us, gently, of our place in the procession of time. Many notable writers of the nineteenth and early twentieth centuries—Samuel Taylor Coleridge, Robert Southey, Beatrix Potter—found inspiration there, but none more famously than poet William Wordsworth, who was both a native and longtime resident. While living there, he wrote many famous poems in which he captured the region's soothing effect, its ability to make us feel moored to something beautiful, protective, and timeless. "Come forth into the light of things," he urged in "The Tables Turned;" "Let Nature be your teacher."

Basil
Pine
Bottle green
Truffle
Soulful
Intimate
Comforting
Umber
Moss
Hunter
Devoted
Intuitive
Accepting
Innate
Sepia
Alligator
Saddle
Forgiving
Coppice
Mindful
Protective
Sustaining
Nurturing
Grounded
Bison
Sorrel
Fern
Mushroom

Anthology

There is no better way to personalize our homes than with the artifacts of our lives: photographs, objects acquired from travels, inherited furniture, and art. The most powerful of these artifacts, and the ones we cherish most, are those that conjure a place and time to which we are connected in some meaningful way. The only rule of thumb in displaying these items is to give them positions of distinction befitting their significance to us, regardless of their sophistication or monetary worth.

When my husband, Mike, and I married and moved in together, he brought with him a collection of valuable antique maps he had assembled over the years. He loved them because they were all maps of Cheshire, the county in northern England where he grew up. Although faded from age, they were rendered in the colors of the land they depicted: leaf green, gray, and shades of brown. They bore sepia-toned ink markings, some legible, some not, and they were framed in wood from the Cheshire region. I brought with me a collection of stones from the many places I had visited, which I picked up free of charge from the ground in their countries of origin. Their colors too, although less varied than Mike's maps, bore the colors of the worlds they came from: the soil, the mud, the lake bottoms.

We made no attempt to separate Mike's collectors' items from my rocks; equally evocative of times and places we wished to remember, we displayed both collections prominently in our dining room—the maps on the wall, the stones lining the windowsills. The most effective design schemes I have seen take similar liberties with collected objects, the function of which is to remind as much as to decorate. Fine art and children's drawings, antique wooden furniture and sleek modern upholstery; precious metals and primitive stone sculptures; and modern fixtures and leather-bound books all work together to tell our stories when they are rooted in our histories and passions. Find and display those things you connect with, and you have a home.

Slumber

Hibernation—that prolonged, deep sleep through the barren months of the year—captivates the human imagination. Animals that hibernate spend the plentiful months gorging to build fat (the black bear can gain as much as thirty pounds a week during this time) and preparing their nests. They spend the dark cold months sleeping so soundly that, for many, no amount of motion, jostling, or noise can awaken them. Their core body temperatures drop precipitously; their pulse rates plummet; and their breathing slows drastically.

Scientists who study hibernation, though, are no longer certain that those long winter's naps are for animals only. More than one hundred years ago, an article in the *British Medical Journal* reported that a population of Russians in the Pskov region, where winter food supplies were nearly nonexistent, slept for six months of the year, waking once a day to eat a bite of bread and down a sip of water before returning to sleep. The same practice was observed among French peasants in the 1800s. More recent studies have focused on whether all humans have the ability to hibernate, if necessary, to survive extreme conditions. And some observers wonder aloud if we weren't all meant to meet the challenges of short days and cold temperatures with blissful sleep, which is certainly tempting.

"In addition to the economic advantages of hibernation, the mere thought of a sleep that knits up the raveled sleeve of care for half a year on end is calculated to fill our harassed souls with envy."

—*British Medical Journal*, 1900

What
We Touch

When I was young, my father would often drive
with me into Manhattan to visit the Metropolitan
Museum of Art. I knew that touching the artwork
was prohibited, but I did it anyway when I thought
the guards weren't looking. I believed that if I
touched the objects into which these artists had
poured their creativity, it would rub off on me. I
was caught a few times and chastised appropriately,
but the guards did that with a smile on their faces.
Even with a job to do, they understood the desire to
connect with the things that move us.

"It is not so much for its beauty that the forest makes a claim upon men's hearts, as for that subtle something, that quality of air that emanates from old trees, that so wonderfully changes and renews a weary spirit."

—ROBERT LOUIS STEVENSON, from "Forest Notes," *Thoughts on Walking,* 1875

Reclaimed Wood

One of the most dramatic and sustainable ways to add character and depth to a home is through the use of salvaged wood. Oak, beech, maple, walnut, and pine all have a broad range of grains. The colors of these woods range from lighter ash to the deepest umber and can work in any home. The more interesting the grain and knot, the larger plank size should be used.

Whichever wood you do choose, it will have a history, evident in the marks of age and usage—the worn areas, cracks, old nail holes—that give it interest and authenticity. Used in new construction, salvaged wood adds soul to a home that modern materials often lack. It is beautiful in exposed beams, as flooring, as fireplace mantels, or in tables or countertops. Through refinishing, wood can acquire whatever color and patina you prefer, although I prefer a finish that is as close as possible to its inherent color.

Wood can be reclaimed from a variety of sources. Salvage yards are an efficient way to canvass for old wood, but you can acquire some materials without a middleman with a little legwork. Dilapidated barns are a good source of wood planking; talk to their owners to see if they are willing to part with it. Shipping companies may have stashes of old wood crates that can be purchased and repurposed, and boatyards are a promising source of teak, a particularly rustic and durable wood.

Katagami

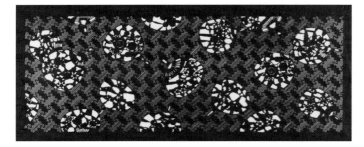

Katagami are Japanese paper stencils traditionally used for printing kimono fabric. The making of the stencils, an art form no longer commonly practiced, requires extensive training and immense skill. The word *katagami* derives from *kata*, meaning "pattern" or "template," and *gami*, meaning "paper." This tradition is more than a thousand years old and has long been associated with the Ise Province.

Katagami has always been a fusion of nature's gifts and human artistry. The stencils are constructed of three paper layers, made from the bark of the mulberry tree. The paper is coated with the juice of tannin-rich persimmon, which gives it a deep brown color. It is then hung in a closed room and smoked for several days to harden the persimmon coating, a process that can produce an intensely brown, almost mahogany, surface that is insect- and water-resistant.

Highly skilled craftsmen using sharp cutting tools painstakingly carve these treated papers, often in stunningly detailed motifs and images. Once they have completed their pattern, a silk thread net (which replaced the use of human hair) is laminated onto the back of the stencil to stabilize and reinforce the design during printing. Dye-resistant rice paste is passed repeatedly through the openings in the stencils onto cloth, until the cloth is evenly covered in the motif. The cloth is dyed and the paste is washed out (a technique known as *katazome*) to reveal the patterned fabric.

Katagami stencils are in most instances all that remain of this beautiful textile printing tradition, as few of the fabrics themselves survive. In 2014, the Kunstgewerbe Museum in Dresden, Germany, rediscovered ninety-two boxes of *katagami* that had languished in storage for one hundred twenty-five years. The boxes contained some fifteen thousand stencils, making it the largest collection in the world.

Katagami stencils tell us not only about the artistry and effort that the Japanese poured into their textile creations, but also, in their motifs, about what they valued as a people. Many of their patterns are inspired by nature: bamboo, rain, butterflies, and cherry blossoms, for instance. Others are familial or folkloric: heraldic symbols and family crests, images from literature and legend. Still others are composed of abstract geometric shapes, whose apparent meaning lies in their beauty alone.

Scentiment

Smell is the oldest of our senses. It is intertwined, biologically, with the emotion and memory centers of our brains as part of the limbic system, giving smell a uniquely powerful hold on us. This comes at a cost: while visual images are processed through many different parts of the brain and are easily translated into language, scent is far more difficult to describe. Many of us lack the vocabulary to articulate what we smell and are able to identify a scent based solely on its associations. Ozone and petrichor are fragrant, often pleasantly so, but most of us would simply call them "summer rain." You might be detecting jasmonic acid or green leaf volatiles, but you are far more likely to declare, with a smile, that you smell fresh cut grass.

Science tells us that the scents of our childhoods—those we encounter in the first five years of life—evoke the most vivid memories and emotions. And the most beloved of these fragrances share a theme. They are the smells of hearth and home, and this is what we call them: baking bread, fresh laundry, aftershave, a Sunday roast, freshly brewed coffee, Christmas trees, bacon, log fires, leather, vanilla extract, a clean home, our mother's perfume, and, yes, newly cut grass.

What We Give

Shortly after we were married, my husband, Mike, and I moved out of New York City to a house in northern New Jersey. It was a major change for me—I had spent my entire career in cities—but Mike had a job in New Jersey and we wanted to start a family, so it seemed to make sense. Before we settled in, furnished our home, or made friends there, however, Mike's beloved mother suffered a stroke and slipped into a coma. Upon hearing the news, Mike flew to the United Kingdom, where his family resided. He remained by his mother's side for nearly six weeks straight—brushing her hair, holding her hand, talking to her, and sleeping by her side until her death. She never regained consciousness.

At the time I didn't fully grasp the profound nature of the vigil that Mike was keeping. I was focused on our new unfurnished house in the suburbs, where I knew no one, and adjusting to a commuter's existence. I was a newlywed whose ideas of married bliss were, temporarily at least, unrealized. And my own immediate family was healthy, intact, and nearby. I had not, to that point, been called upon to put love into action. All I could do was observe.

The significance of Mike's devotion to his mother, and later, to his father, has revealed itself to me slowly over the years, as we have raised our daughters and built our lives around dear friends and family, some of whom are now gone. He knew long before I did that we are bound most tightly to those we love by what we give to them.

Acknowledgments

First and foremost, I must give thanks to Dorothy Mitchell, who was able, time after time, to take my gibberish and transform it into richer, far more coherent prose. She is the smartest person I know, and her devotion to this book and our friendship—well, I cannot express in eloquent enough language without her assistance! But if I were to create a fabric of Dorothy, it would be a perfect blending of all my favorite colors. Thank you too to her family—Stanton, Gemma, and Ty—for loaning her to me.

I am so grateful for the tremendous support of all my colleagues, who help to make my work a success and allow me to be a "creative" as a profession. Thank you to all my partners at Pollack Weitzner, especially Rick and Susan Sullivan, whose belief in me has enabled me to write this book. Thank you to all our employees and sales representatives past and present, who are out there every day getting Weitzner products into people's hands and spaces.

To my treasured second family at Samuel and Sons: I am glad we met each other those many years ago in Los Angeles. My deep thanks to: Christoph Haussler, for taking the chance on a female American to design for a male-dominant German fabric company; Tom Boller and Trish Hay, my mentors; everyone at Katsu, for all their support and belief; Art Libera for his treasured wisdom; Lori Weitzner Design board members and adopted siblings, Ivan Casamassima and Victor Wong; and Kathryn Kimball, who was the first to encourage me to go out and lecture about my inspirations so many years ago. I'd also like to thank all my extraordinarily talented clients and friends who somehow always make magic with what I throw at them and who continue to support my work so gallantly: Roger Thomas, Suryati Benniardi, Marc Thee, Penny Drue Baird, Ben Aguilar, Lisa Staprans, Mia Jung, Gary Wheeler, and so many others.

My thanks to Spread PR, who always manages to get my work into the right places, and to Margaret Russell, Michael Boodro, Cindy Allen, Karen Marx, and all the other editors who have so generously showcased my work in their luminous publications.

To my team at Lori Weitzner Design Studio, I cherish you: David Harris, for being a most generous and smart adviser, mentor, and source of support; Sumitra Mattai and Emily Yurkevicz, for their endless creativity, patience, and assistance; and most of all, Nina Chidichimo, an essential contributor to this book. Her dedication to researching, resourcing, gathering, and organizing material, and keeping me in check has been integral at every turn. I deeply appreciate her hard work, input, upbeat attitude, and always ready and heartfelt smile.

I am honored to showcase the work of the most talented photographers I know—Antonis Achilleos, Scott Jones, Pamela Viola, and Amos Chan—as well as the many others included in this book.

My thanks to those whose early counsel helped me bring my idea into a visual shape: to Chris Evans for his advice; to Krista Stack for her fact-finding missions; to my cherished friend Jan Baker, graphic designer and professor extraordinaire, who radiates creativity and generosity, for her keen guidance; and to Jan's talented students at the Rhode Island School of Design who participated in a project using some of the editorial content from the book.

Thank you, Steven Holt: I know you are in heaven now looking down proudly. Thank you for making me think more deeply at every turn. And to my mom—who has just arrived in heaven—I'm sorry you never got to see the final book, but I know you would be proud.

To my personal friends who are always there for me: my soul sisters, Ellen Abrams, Elizabeth Dane, and Jodi Serota, and my soul brother, Rocky La Fleur; Llorraine Neithardt, for her all-knowing insights and guidance; Susan Sterman Jones and Jan Davis, for sticking with me since kindergarten; David Handelman, for always challenging me; Monique King, for reminding me of the importance of having a good time; Ann Duffy and Paul Mattison, Liz Fraser and Patrick Killacky, for being surrogate family members; Jessica Koenigsberg, my yoga guru; Epsie Sewell, for keeping the kids clean and happy; and to Will Papp, who has taught me how to truly appreciate nature.

I'd also like to thank art director Lynne Yeamans, designer Niloo Tehranchi, and production director Susan Kosko for helping me create this beautiful book.

Most important, I thank my editor Elizabeth Viscott Sullivan. Without her incredible generosity, this book would not exist. Her support has been incomparable. Her giving of her time and guidance has taught me how to stay authentic.

And finally, of course, to Mike, Emma, and Sophie. You make me want to be a better person every day.

Select Bibliography

BOOKS

Alexander, Victoria. *Colour: A Journey*. London: Murdoch Books, 2012.

Andrieu, Philippe. *Ladurée Sucré: The Sweet Recipes*. Chene, 2011.

Bartlett, John, and Geoffrey O'Brien. *Bartlett's Familiar Quotations*. Boston, MA: Little, Brown, 2012.

Bernstein, Peter. *The Power of Gold: The History of an Obsession*. New York: John Wiley & Sons, Inc., 2004.

Bloom, Harold. Shakespeare: *The Invention of the Human*. New York: Riverhead Books, 1998.

Blumenberg, Hans. *Paradigms for a Metaphorology*. trans. Robert Savage (1960; repr., Ithaca, NY: Cornell University Press, 2010).

Boas, Franz. *Handbook of American Indian Languages*. Washington: G.P.O., 1911.

Campbell, Joseph, and Bill Moyers. *The Power of Myth*. New York: Doubleday, 1988.

Casadio, Mariuccia. *Emilio Pucci*. New York: Universe Publishing, 1998.

Casson, Lionel. *Ancient Egypt*. New York: Time, Inc., 1965.

Conran, Terence. *Conran on Color*. London: Octopus Group, 2015.

Delbanco, Nicholas. *The Art of Youth: Crane, Carrington, Gershwin and the Nature of First Acts*. Seattle: Lake Union Publishing, 2003.

Dahl, Roald, and Quentin Blake. *Charlie and the Great Glass Elevator*. New York: Puffin, 2007.

De La Mare, Walter. *The Complete Poems of Walter De La Mare*. London: Faber, 1975.

Delaunay, Sonia, Elizabeth Morano, and Diana Vreeland. Sonia Delaunay: *Art into Fashion*. New York: George Braziller, 1986.

Dog, Tieraona Low, Rebecca L. Johnson, Stephen Foster, and David Kiefer. *National Geographic Guide to Medicinal Herbs: The World's Most Effective Healing Plants*. Washington, D.C.: National Geographic, 2012.

Eliot, Marc. *Walt Disney: Hollywood's Dark Prince*. New York: Carol Publishing Group, 1993.

Finlay, Victoria. *Color: A Natural History of the Palette*. New York: Random House Trade Paperbacks, 2003.

Fleming, John V. *The Dark Side of the Enlightenment: Wizards, Alchemists and Spiritual Seekers in the Age of Reason*. New York: W.W. & Norton Co., 2013.

Fussell, Paul. Uniforms: *Why We Are What Wear*. New York: Houghton Mifflin, 2002.

Geisel, Theodor Seuss. *The Beginnings of Dr. Seuss, An Informal Reminiscence*. Hanover, NH: Dartmouth College, 2004.

Grant, Michael, and John Hazel. *Gods and Mortals in Classic Mythology*. Springfield, MA: G&C Merriam Co., 1973.

Graves, Robert. *The Greek Myths: I*. London: Penguin Books, 1960.

Juster, Norton. *The Phantom Tollbooth*. London: Collins, 1999.

Krauss, Lawrence. *A Universe from Nothing: Why There Is Something Rather Than Nothing*. New York: Free Press (2012).

Kunz, George Frederick, and Charles Hugh Stevens. *The Book of the Pearl: The History, Art, Science, and Industry of the Queen of Gems*. New York: The Century Co., 1908.

Kuo, Susanna, Richard L. Wilson, and Thomas S. Michie. *Carved Paper: The Art of Japanese Stencils*. Santa Barbara, CA: Santa Barbara Museum of Art, 1998.

Ladinsky, Daniel James. *Love Poems from God: Twelve Sacred Voices from the East and West*. New York: Penguin Compass, 2002.

Lavignac, Albert. *Music and Musicians*. New York: Henry Holt, 1903.

Mackellar, Dorothea. *My Country and Other Poems*. Ringwood, Victoria, Australia: Viking O'Neil, 1993.

Milne, A. A., and Ernest H. Shepard. *When We Were Very Young*. New York: Dutton, 1961.

Nabakov, Vladmir. *Speak, Memory: An Autobiography Revisited*. New York: Vintage International, 1989.

Paoletti, Jo B. P*ink and Blue: Telling the Girls from the Boys in America*. Bloomington, IN: Indiana University Press, 2012.

Pastoureau, Michel. *Blue: The History of a Color*. Princeton, NJ: Princeton University Press, 2001 (trans).

Perelman, Dale. *The Regent*. Bloomington, IN: AuthorHouse, 2012.

Pitman, Joanna. *On Blondes*. New York: Bloomsbury, 2003.

Post, Emily. *Etiquette in Society, in Business, in Politics and at Home*. New York: Funk & Wagnalls Co., 1922.

Ronnberg, Ami, and Kathleen Martin, eds. *The Book of Symbols*. Köln: Taschen, 2010.

Roome, Loretta. Mehndi: *The Timeless Art of Henna Painting*. New York: St. Martin's Press, 1998.

Rowling, J. K. *Harry Potter and the Prisoner of Azkaban*. New York: Scholastic, Inc., 2001.

Sandburg, Carl. *The Complete Poems of Carl Sandburg*. San Diego: Harcourt, Brace, 1970.

Schiff, David. Gershwin: *Rhapsody in Blue*. Cambridge, England: Cambridge University Press, 1997.

Shakespeare, William, and Alfred Harbage, eds. *The Complete Works*. New York: Viking Press, 1977.

Smith, Gavin D. *The Lake Poets*. Gloucestershire: Amberley, 2013.

Streeter, Edwin. *The Great Diamonds of the World, Their History and Romance*, 1882.

Thoreau, Henry David. *Walden*. Las Vegas, NV: Empire, 2012.

———— and Bradford Torrey, eds. *The Writings of Henry David Thoreau: Journal, Vol. II*. Boston: Houghton Mifflin, 1906.

Van Campen, Cretien. *The Hidden Sense: Synesthesia in Art and Science*. Cambridge, MA: The MIT Press, 2010.

Whiteley, Opal. *Opal*. New York: Three Rivers, 1995.

Weir, Caroline, and Robin Weir. *Ice Creams, Sorbets and Gelatis: The Definitive Guide*. London: Grub Street, 2010.

ARTICLES

"Alexander McQueen." *Vogue* (March 9, 2010). Accessed January 7, 2016. www.vogue.co.uk/fashion/autumn-winter-2010/ready-to-wear/alexander-mcqueen.

Alexander, J. Wesley. "History of the Medical Use of Silver." *Surgical Infections*, Vol. 10, No. 3 (2009). Accessed November 14, 2015. www.tse.colloidalsilverkillsviruses.com/pdf/history.pdf.

Barringer, Taylor. *Elle.com*. "The History of Red Lipstick." Accessed March 5, 2015. http://www.elle.com/beauty/makeup-skin-care/tips/g8050/red-lipstick/?slide=1.

Blake, Judith. "Cracker Jack: Peanuts and a Prize." *Seattle Times* (March 30, 2005). Accessed December 28, 2015. www.seattletimes.com/life/food-drink/cracker-jack-peanuts-and-a-prize/.

"A Brief History of Crooning." *Financial Times* (April 28, 2007). Accessed November 13, 2015. www.ft.com/intl/cms/s/0/02eae76a-f5a7-11db-a3fe-000b5df10621.html.

Choi, Charles. "Eye-Trackers Help Scientists Study How Peacock Tails Lure Peahens." *Washington Post*. (August 12, 2013). Accessed November 27, 2015. www.washingtonpost.com/national/health-science/eye-trackers-help-scientists-study-how-peacock-tails-lure-peahens/2013/08/12/a01f7b54-f622-11e2-9434-60440856fadf_story.html.

Crompton, Sarah. "Top Hats Off to the Dancer Other Dancers Envy." *The Telegraph* (April 9, 2012). Accessed July 1, 2015. www.telegraph.co.uk/culture/theatre/dance/9193951/Top-hats-off-to-the-dancer-other-dancers-envy.html.

Deardorff, Julie. "Some Antibacterials Come with Worrisome Silver Lining," *Chicago Tribune* (February 16, 2014). Accessed November 13, 2015. articles.chicagotribune.com/2014-02-16/health/ct-nanosilver-met-20140216_1_consumer-products-other-antibiotic-drugs-germs.

Dobnik, Varena. "Revelers Participate in Annual Easter Day Parade on Fifth Avenue." *News 4 New York* (March 31, 2013). Accessed December 22, 2015. www.nbcnewyork.com/news/local/NYC-Celebrates-Easter-Fun-Parade-5th-Avenue-St-Patricks-Cathedral-200794531.html.

Dobson, Roger, and Abul Taher. "Corrected – Cave Girls Were First Blondes to Have Fun." *The Sunday Times*. (February 26, 2006). Accessed December 4, 2015. The Sunday Times Digital Archive.

Fields, Helen. "Fragrant Flashbacks: Smells Rouse Early Memories." *Observer* Vol. 25, No. 4, April, 2012. Accessed August 13, 2015. www.psychologicalscience.org/index.php/publications/observer/2012/april-12/fragrant-flashbacks.html.

Fricke, David. "Shadows in the Night." *Rolling Stone* (February 3, 2015). Accessed November 10, 2015. www.rollingstone.com/music/albumreviews/bob -dylan-shadows-in-the-night-20150203.

Galchen, Rivka. "The Melancholy Mystery of Lullabies." *New York Times* (October 14, 2015). Accessed October 31, 2015. www.nytimes.com/2015/10/18/ magazine/the-melancholy-mystery-of-lullabies .html?_r=0.

Geiling, Natasha. "The Science Behind Honey's Eternal Shelf Life," *Smithsonian.com* (August 22, 2013). Accessed February 10, 2015. www.smithsonianmag .com/science-nature/the-science-behind-honeys -eternal-shelf-life-1218690/?no-ist.

Govan, Fiona. "Treasure Hunters Ordered to Return £250m of Loot to Spain." *The Telegraph* (June 4, 2009). Accessed October 24, 2015. www.telegraph. co.uk/news/worldnews/europe/spain/5444134/ Treasure-hunters-ordered-to-pay-Spain-350m-for -gold-coins.html.

Gray, Christopher. "Streetscapes/52nd Street and Fifth Avenue; The Jeweler That Conquered a Millionaire's Row." *New York Times* (January 28, 2001). Accessed November 28, 2015. www.nytimes.com/2001 /01/28/realestate/streetscapes-52nd -street-fifth-avenue-jeweler-that-conquered -millionaire-s-row.html.

Handwerk, Brian. "Artificial Spider Silk Could Be Used for Armor, More." *National Geographic* (January14, 2005). Accessed November 5, 2015. news .nationalgeographic.com/news/2005/01/ 0114_050114_tv_spider.html.

Hazen, Robert. "What Makes Diamond Sparkle?" *Nova* (February 1, 2000). Accessed November 11, 2015. www.pbs.org/wgbh/nova/physics/diamond -science.html.

Hegarty, Stephanie. "How Jeans Conquered the World." *BBC News Magazine* (February 28, 2012). Accessed October 13, 2015. www.bbc.com/news/ magazine-17101768.

Heinsohn, Robert. "Why Are Male Birds More Colorful Than Female Birds?" *Scientific American* (September 12, 2005). Accessed November 27, 2015. www.scientificamerican.com/article/why-are -male-birds-more-c/.

Hill, Norman E. "The Arizona Biltmore Resort and Spa—A Historical Icon Flourishing with Time." *Business Insider* (December 1, 2011). AccessedDecember 1, 2015. www .businessinsider.com/the-arizona -biltmore-resort-and-spaa-historical -icon-flourishing-with-time-2011-12.

"Human Hibernation." *British Medical Journal* (May 6, 2000), 320(7244): 1245. Accessed November 14, 2015. www.ncbi.nlm.nih.gov/pmc/articles/ PMC1117993/.

Jamie, Kathleen. "Sonia Delaunay: The Avant-Garde Queen of Loud, Wearable Art." *The Guardian* (March 27, 2015). Accessed December 29, 2015. www.theguardian.com/artanddesign/2015/mar/27/ sonia-delaunay-avant-garde-queen-art-fashion -vibrant-tate-modern.

Joyce, Christopher. "Spider Wranglers Weave One-of- a-Kind Web." *NPR* (September 27, 2009). Accessed November 12, 2014. www.npr.org/templates/ story/story.php?storyId=113223398.

Loftus, Geoff. "The Keys of Walt Disney's Mickey Mouse Leadership." *Forbes* (May 22 2014). Accessed November 2, 2015. www.forbes .com/sites/geoffloftus/2014/05/22/ mickey-mouse-leadership/.

Kaiser, Tiffany. "Spider Silk Used to Make 'Bulletproof' Human Skin." *Daily Tech* (August 18, 2011). Accessed November 2, 2015. www.dailytech.com/Spider +Silk+Used+to+Make+Bulletproof+Human+Skin/ article22482.htm

King, Steve. "Naked Lustre." *Vanity Fair* (July, 2009). Accessed November 2, 2015. www.vanityfair.com/ news/2009/07/pearl-industry200907.

Klara, Thomas. "How Tiffany's Iconic Box Became the World's Most Popular Package; This Robin's Egg Blue Is Trademarked." *AdWeek* (September 22, 2014). Accessed January 19, 2015. www.adweek .com/news/advertising-branding/how-tiffany-s -iconic-box-became-world-s-most-popular -package-160228.

Knirsch, Christian. "World Metaphor, Metametaphor: Veils in Literature, Literature as Veil." *Journal of Comparative Studies of South Asia, Africa, and the Middle East*, Vol. 32, No. 1. Durham, NC: Duke University Press, 2012.

Kriegsman, Alan. "For Dancers, A Peerless Model." Washington Post (June 23, 1987). Accessed December 4, 2015. *ProQuest. Web.*

Lineberry, Cate. "Diamonds Unearthed." *Smithsonian.com* (December 2006). Accessed November 3, 2014. www.smithsonianmag .com/science-nature/diamonds-unearthed-141629226/?no-ist=&page=2.

"Logical Rain: Rediscovered After 125 Years in Dresden: The World's Richest Resource of Japanese Stencils for Dyeing Samurai Kimonos." *Staatliche Kunstsammlungen Dresden.* Accessed January 4, 2016. www.skd.museum/en/special-exhibitions/archive/ logical-rain/index.html.

Maglaty, Jeanne. "When Did Girls Start Wearing Pink?" *Smithsonian.com* (April 7, 2011). Accessed October 13, 2015. www.smithsonianmag.com/arts-culture/ when-did-girls-start-wearing-pink-1370097/?no-ist.

Mandel, Jonah. "The Color Techelet." *The Jerusalem Post* (March 4, 2011). Accessed December 2, 2015. www.jpost.com/JewishWorld/JewishNews/ Article.aspx?id=210753.

Miller, Diane Disney. "My Dad, Walt Disney: Disney's Folly." *Saturday Evening Post* (December 22, 1956). Accessed December 23, 2105. www.saturdayeveningpost.com/wp-content/ uploads/satevepost/Disneys-Folly1.pdf.

Mishan, Ligaya. "Airy Macarons That Rise Above the Rest." *New York Times* (November 1, 2011).

Mone, Gregory. "20 Things You Didn't Know About ... Hibernation." *Discover Magazine* (March 2013). Accessed November 10, 2015. discovermagazine .com/2013/march/21-20-things-hibernation.

Morin, Monte. "Silver Found to Increase Effectiveness of Antibiotics." *L.A. Times* (June 20, 2013). Accessed October 27, 2015. www.articles.latimes.com/2013/ jun/20/science/la-sci-antibiotics-silver-20130620.

Morris, Bernadine. "Emilio Pucci, Designer of Bright Prints, Dies at 78." *New York Times* (December 1, 1992). Accessed November 27, 2015. www.nytimes .com/1992/12/01/nyregion/emilio-pucci -designer-of-bright-prints-dies-at-78.html.

Mower, Sarah. "Fall 2010 Ready-to-Wear: Alexander McQueen." *Vogue* (March 8, 2010). Accessed January 7, 2016. www.vogue.com/fashion-shows/ fall-2010-ready-to-wear/alexander-mcqueen.

Murphy, Bill Jr. "12 Moving Facts About Walt Disney That Will Inspire You to Succeed." *Inc.* (October 1, 2015). Accessed November 27, 2015. www.inc.com/ bill-murphy-jr/13-moving-facts-about-walt-disney -that-will-inspire-you-to-succeed.html.

"Navy Blue." *The American Heritage Illustrated Encyclopedic Dictionary.* Boston: Houghton Mifflin, 1987.

Nugent, Frank S. "Movie Review: Snow White and the Seven Dwarfs." *New York Times* (January 14, 1938). Accessed November 2, 2015. www.nytimes .com/movie/review?res=EE05E7DF173FE070BC4C 52DFB7668383629EDE.

O'Connell, Sanjida. "How Did the Peacock Get His Tail?" *National Geographic* (September 9, 2002), from *The Independent* (London). Accessed November 27, 2015. http://news.nationalgeographic.com/ news/2002/09/0909_peacock_2.html.

Orci, Taylor. "The Original 'Blonde Bombshell' Used Actual Bleach on Her Head." *The Atlantic* (February 22, 2013). Accessed February 15, 2015. www.theatlantic.com/health/archive/2013/02/ the-original-blonde-bombshell-used-actual-bleach -on-her-head/273333/.

"Origin of Navy Terminology: Navy Blue." *Naval History and Heritage Command.* Accessed October 29, 2105. www.history.navy.mil/research/library/online -reading-room/title-list-alphabetically/o/origin -navy-terminology.html.

Parsons, Russ. "Cracker Jack: 120-Year-Old Junk Food Gets New Flavors, 'Enhanced' Prizes." *L.A. Times* (June 4, 2103). Accessed December 28, 2105. www .latimes.com/food/dailydish/la-dd-cracker-jack -updated-new-flavors-20130604-story.html.

Perry, Nina. "The Universal Language of Lullabies." *BBC* (January 21, 2013). Accessed October 30, 2015. www.bbc.com/news/magazine-21035103.

Rhodes, Jesse. "For Those Ruby Red Slippers, There's No Place Like Home." *Smithsonian.com* (January 2009). Accessed January 7, 2016. www .smithsonianmag.com/arts-culture/for-those-ruby -red-slippers-theres-no-place-like-home-130170740/.

Robson, David. "There Really Are 50 Eskimo Words for Snow." *Washington Post* (January 14, 2013), reprinted from *New Scientist* (December 18, 2012). Accessed November 24, 2014. www.washingtonpost.com/national/health -science/there-really-are-50-eskimo-words-for -snow/2013/01/14/e0e3f4e0- 59a0-11e2-beee-6e38f5215402_story.html.

"The Rules for Mourning Are Those of Good Taste." *Vogue* (June 1, 1922). Accessed December 4, 2015. *ProQuest. Web.*

Rundle, Rhonda L. "This War Against Germs Has a Silver Lining." *Wall Street Journal* (June 6, 2006). Accessed December 16, 2015. www.wsj.com/articles/ SB114955908525572199.

Sakal, Mike. "A Cracker Jack of a Tradition: 100 Years of Prizes in Every Box." *East Valley Tribune* (July 27, 2102). Accessed December 27, 2015. www.eastvalleytribune.com/columns/east_ valley_voices/article_4082a658-d783-11e1-a5ef -001a4bcf887a.html.

Salter, Kate. "Sonia Delaunay: A Life of Contrasts." *The Telegraph* (July 31, 2011). Accessed December 30, 2016. www.telegraph.co.uk/culture/art/art -features/8668887/Sonia-Delaunay-a-life-of -contrasts.html.

Simmons, Walter. "That's How Navy Uniforms Were Born." *Chicago Tribune* (October 31, 1943). Accessed November 1, 2015. http://archives.chicagotribune .com/1943/10/31/page/154/article/thats-how -navy-uniforms-were-born.

Stacy, Mitch. "17 Tons of Shipwrecked Silver Head for Spain on Two Planes." *NBCNews.com* (February 24, 2012). Accessed February 16, 2015. www.nbcnews .com/id/46514441/ns/us_news-life/t/tons -shipwrecked-silver-head-spain-two-planes/#. VOyRkE05A5s.

Tyson, Peter. "Bear Essentials of Hibernation." *Nova* (December 18, 2000). Accessed November 26, 2015. www.pbs.org/wgbh/nova/nature/bear-essentials-of -hibernation.html.

"Underwater Cultural Heritage, Convention on the Protection of the Underwater Cultural Heritage Will Enter into Force in January 2009." *UNESCO .org*. Accessed November 21, 2015. www.ioc-unesco. org/index.php?option=com_content&view=article &id=83:underwater-cultural-heritage&catid=14&It emid=100063.

Walsh, Paul. "Crayola Marks 64-Count Box's 50th Birthday with New Colors." *Star Tribune* (April 10, 2008). Accessed December 23, 2015. www.startribune.com/crayola-marks-64-count -box-s-50th-birthday-with-new-colors/17459559/.

"The Wealth of Ancient Egypt." *The British Museum.* Accessed December 2, 2015. www.britishmuseum .org/PDF/AncientEgypt_TeachersNotes.pdf.

The Week Staff. "Military Breakthrough: 'Bulletproof' Skin Made from Spider Silk." *The Week* (August 19, 2011). http://theweek.com/articles/482397/ military-breakthrough-bulletproof-skin-made -from-spider-silk.

Yuhas, Daisy. "Storm Scents: It's True, You Can Smell Oncoming Summer Rain." *Scientific American* (July 18, 2012). Accessed November 27, 2015. www.scientificamerican.com/article/storm-scents -smell-rain/.

OTHER SOURCES

"About Emilio Pucci." *Emilio Pucci.com.* Accessed November 27, 2015. www.home.emiliopucci.com/ about-emilio-pucci.

"Biography: Dr. Seuss." *Scholastic.* Accessed November 27, 2015. www.scholastic.com/teachers/ contributor/dr-seuss.

Colgan, Deirdre. "City Guide to Sacred Spaces – New York, N.Y.: Manhattan and Brooklyn." PBS/ Sacred Spaces International, 2010. Accessed November 28, 2015. www-tc.pbs .org/godinamerica/art/nyc_ cityguide.pdf.

Downey, Lynn. "A Short History of Denim." 2014. Accessed October 27, 2015. *Levi Strauss & Co.* www.levistrauss.com/wp-content/uploads/2014/01/A-Short-History-of-Denim2.pdf.

"Erol Becker Chapel of the Good Shepherd." *St. Peter's Church.* Accessed November 11, 2015. www.saintpeters.org/the-arts-and-design/art-collection/nevelson/.

"Explore Colors." *Crayola.* Accessed November 27, 2015. www.crayola.com/explore-colors.aspx.

"Fun Facts." *American Bee Journal.* Accessed October 19, 2015. www.americanbeejournal.com/site/epage/79348_828.htm.

Hale, James (Dir.). *David Bowie & the Story of Ziggy Stardust.* BBC Four (2012). Documentary film.

"History of the Ladurée Macaron." *Ladurée.* Accessed November 28, 2015. https://fabricantdedouceurs.laduree.com/en_fr/#!brand/history.

"History of the Levi's 501 Jeans." *Levi Strauss & Co.* Accessed October 27, 2015. lsco.s3.amazonaws.com/wp-content/uploads/2014/01/History-of-Levis-501-Jeans.pdf.

"Imaging of Egyptian Blue." *The British Museum.* Accessed November 23, 2015. https://www.britishmuseum.org/pdf/Imaging%20of%20Egyptian%20Blue_Technical%20details.pdf.

"Interview with Mikhail Baryshnikov," transcript. *CNN Larry King Weekend* (May 5, 2002). http://www.cnn.com/TRANSCRIPTS/0205/05/lklw.00.html.

"Is There Gold in the Ocean?" National Ocean Service. Accessed February 10, 2015. oceanservice.noaa.gov/facts/gold.html.

"Jacob Davis: His Life and Contributions." *Levi Strauss & Co.* Accessed October 27, 2015. http://www.levistrauss.com/our-story/.

Lauchlan, Archie (Dir). *The Wonderful World of Technicolor.* BBC Scotland (aired December 25, 2008).

The Metropolitan Museum of Art. "Costume Institute's Fall Exhibition Focuses on Victorian and Edwardian Mourning Attire." New York: News Release (October 20, 2014).

The Metropolitan Museum of Art. "Death Becomes Her: A Century of Mourning Attire, October 21, 2014 – February 1, 2015, Image Identifications." New York: News Release.

Muriel, Barbier. "Diamond, Known as the 'Regent.'" *Louvre.* Accessed October 28, 2015. www.louvre.fr/en/oeuvre-notices/diamond-known-regent.

"Nyx." *Encyclopaedia Brittanica.* Accessed January 16, 2015. www.britannica.com/EBchecked/topic/423288/Nyx.

"Our Story." *Levi Strauss & Co.* Accessed October 27, 2015. www.levistrauss.com/our-story/.

Palmer, Robin and Jennifer Fox. "More to Explore" (Diamonds). *National Geographic* (March 1, 2002). Accessed January 18, 2015. www.ngm.nationalgeographic.com/ngm/data/2002/03/01/html/ft_20020301.1.htm.

"Properties of Diamonds." *Natural History Museum* (London). Accessed November 4, 2014. www.nhm.ac.uk/nature-online/earth/rock-minerals/diamonds/diamond-properties/.

"Resort History." *Arizona Biltmore.* Accessed December 1, 2015. www.arizonabiltmore.com/about-the-biltmore/resort-history/.

Saarman, Emily. "Symposium Looks at Therapeutic Benefits of Musical Rhythm." *Stanford News Service* (May 31, 2006). Accessed November 28, 2015. http://news.stanford.edu/pr/2006/pr-brainwave-053106.html.

Photography Credits

Achilleos, Antonis: 169; 231, bottom right; 242: © Antonis Achilleos.

Art Resource: 116–117: (Bridgeman-Giraudon/Art Resource, NY); 206–207: (Neue Galerie New York/Art Resource, NY).

Baker, Jan: 138: © Jan Baker.

Barton, Anne-Marie: 163, top left; 231, bottom left: © David Livingston Photography. 238: © Scott Zimmerman. All images courtesy of Anne-Marie Barton.

Bell, Laura: 38–39: © 2006 Laura Bell.

Bridgeman: 155: *Love in Florence*, 1954 (gelatin silver print), Vincenzo Balocchi, (1892–1975), Alinari/Bridgeman Images.

Busink, Tjarko: 125, background; 232–233: © 2013 Tjarko Busink.

Carr, Sayzie: 36–37: © 2015 Sayzie Carr.

Catwalking: 220: © Catwalking.

Chidichimo, Nina: 21, bottom right; 81: © Nina Chidichimo.

Cox, Maria: 135, foreground: © Maria Cox.

Daher Interior Design: 102: © Daher Interior Design, Eric Roth Photography.

Das, Shantanu: 26, foreground: © 2010 Shantanu Das.

Davis Museum: 180: Gift of Mr. Theodore Racoosin, courtesy of Davis Museum at Wellesley College, Wellesley, MA.

Disney Enterprises, Inc.: 189: © 1937 Disney.

Duffy, Ann: 71, foreground: © Ann Duffy.

Duffy Archive Ltd.: 42: Photo Duffy © Duffy Photographer.

Elizabeth Kruger Design: 170: © 2015 Elizabeth Krueger Design. Photograph by Mike Schwartz.

Endless Knot: 142, center: © Endless Knot.

Everett Collection: 58; 66; 80; 104; 125, foreground; 166; 194–195; 198; 212: All images courtesy of the Everett Collection.

Garth, Maria A.: 144–145: © 2015 Maria A. Garth Photography.

Glenn Gissler Design: 190, top and bottom left: © Gross + Daley.

Hamilton, Patrick J.: 230: © 2013 Patrick J. Hamilton.

Hammond, Francis: 84: © Francis Hammond. Courtesy of Dessins LLC.

Hikari, Noora: 18: © 2010 Noora Hikari.

Hillwood Museum: 94, foreground: © Hillwood Estate, Museum, and Gardens, photograph by Ed Owen.

Iacob, Vasile: 113: © 2009 Vasile Iacob.

IBI Designs, Inc.: 164–165, 216: © Photography by Edward Butera/IBI Designs, Inc. Courtesy of Marc-Michaels Interior Design.

Knipstein, R. Brad: 54; 109; 190, bottom right: © R. Brad Knipstein Photography. Courtesy of Lisa Staprans Design.

Lamont, Alexander: 60, bottom left; 234, 236–237: © Alex Lamont.

Lazic, Shannon: 210, top right and bottom left: © Shannon Lazic. Courtesy of Marc-Michaels Interior Design.

Lori Weitzner Design: 10–12; 21, top left; 40–41; 64–65; 67; 71, background; 88–89; 96, background; 114–115; 124; 127; 136–137; 148; 156–157; 173, background; 178–179; 203, background; 204–205; 223–224; 227; 243. *Jennifer Cox*: 2, top; 6. *Scott Jones*: 4; 9, bottom right; 14; 19; 29; 32; 44; 68; 92; 118; 140; 150, top; 160; 184; 208; 228: All images © Lori Weitzner Design.

Macaluso-Williams, Kambriel: 105: 2010 Photo & Midnight Bustle/Mourning Veil by Kambriel.

Maccarrone, Michele: 106: © 2010 Michele Maccarrone.

Minton Redfield, Emily: 163, top right: © Emily Minton Redfield (EMR Photography). Courtesy of Lisa Staprans Design.

Mitchell, Dorothy: 176–177: © Dorothy Mitchell.

Museum of Art, Rhode Island School of Design: 215: *Gloves*, 1933–1937. Attributed to Elsa Schiaparelli. Photography by Erik Gould, courtesy of the Museum of Art, Rhode Island School of Design, Providence; 240 and 241: *Katagami* (hand-cut paper stencil), 19th century. Japanese. Photography by Erik Gould, courtesy of the Museum of Art, Rhode Island School of Design, Providence.

NASA/STScI/WikiSky: 60, top left.

Nilson, Marcus: 83: © Marcus Nilson.

Parinejad, Patricia: 203, top right: © Patricia Parinejad.

Parr, Michael: 100, 152, 226: © Michael Parr.

Penguin Random House: 196: Illustrations from *The Lorax* by Dr. Seuss, ® and copyright © by Dr. Seuss Enterprises, L.P. 1971, renewed 1999. Used by permission of Random House Children's Books, a division of Penguin Random House LLC. All rights reserved.

Perry, Christopher: 90: © 2011 Christopher Perry.

Photofest: 33: Paramount/Photofest.

Piasecki, Eric: 75: © Eric Piasecki/OTTO for Timothy Corrigan.

Pracusa: *Projet de maillot de bain*, Paris, 1928 (watercolor on paper) 27.3 × 20.4 cm (SD 09 345 165 F), Delaunay, Sonia © Pracusa 2016618.

Rowland, Garrett: 2, bottom; 9, top left and top right: © Garrett Rowland.

Sahco: 74; 110, bottom left; 122; 128, top left; 146–147, background; 174; 210, bottom right; 239, left: © Sahco.

Samuel & Sons: 21, bottom left; 61, bottom right; 128, bottom left; 142, bottom left; 163, center left and bottom left; 175; 217, bottom left and bottom right: © Samuel & Sons.

Sargent, Kim: 49, 108, 150 bottom: © Kim Sargent. Courtesy of Marc-Michaels Interior Design.

Shaler Ladd Corporation: 191: © Christian Harder Photography/Shaler Ladd Corporation.

Shutterstock: 34–35: ChameleonsEye/Shutterstock; 72–73: BeautyStockPhoto/Shutterstock. 76–77: Brenda Carson/Shutterstock.

Tate: 24–25 (*Snow Storm-Steam-Boat off a Harbour's Mouth*, 1842, Joseph Mallord William Turner [1775–1851]) © Tate, London 2016.

Thinkstock: 26–27: background a mikos/Thinkstock; 43: Elena Moiseeva/Thinkstock; 46–47: Andreas Krone/Thinkstock; 53: drashokk/Thinkstock; 56–57: moiraff/Thinkstock; 70: XiXinXing/Thinkstock; 85: Dorling Kindersley/Thinkstock; 86–87: kruwt/Thinkstock; 98–99: ShinichiroSaka/Thinkstock; 111: Mcmorabad/Thinkstock; 132: John Foxx/Thinkstock; 146, foreground: AlexPro9500/Thinkstock; 163, bottom right: Steve Baccon/Thinkstock; 167: Photos.com/Thinkstock; 186: Shelly Perry/Thinkstock; 193: KAdams66/Thinkstock; 200, top: Gelia/Thinkstock; 201, bottom: Arsty/Thinkstock.

Thomas Hamel & Associates: 55; 128, bottom right: © Thomas Hamel & Associates, photography by Matt Lowden.

Thompson, Derek: 149: © 2015 Derek Thompson.

Van der Heijden, Franz: 143; 239, center; 239, right: © Frans van der Heijden/Kate Hume.

Viola, Pamela: 16–17; 50–51; 60, bottom right; 94–95, background; 112; 120–121; 130–131; 192; 214, foreground; 235, 244–245: © Pamela H. Viola.

Waldron, William: 23: © William Waldron for Ike Kligerman Barkley.

Warner Brothers: 62: Licensed by Warner Bros. Entertainment Inc. All Rights Reserved.

Weitzner Limited: 21, top right; 48; 61, bottom left; 110, top right; 126; 128, top right; 134–135, background; 142, right; 202, foreground; 202, background; 211; 214, background; 218–219. *Antonis Achilleos:* 13; 20; 60, top right; 61, top left and top right; 96, foreground; 97; 101; 110, bottom right; 129; 133, top left and top right; 133, bottom left and bottom right; 151; 153; 168; 201, top right; 210, top left. *Brad Bloom:* 30–31, background; 31 inset. *Nina Chidichimo:* 158. *Scott Jones:* 52; 110, top left; 162; 200, bottom right; 222–223. All images © Weitzner Limited.

Weitzner, Lori: 8; 9, bottom left; 78; 79, left and right; 123; 158, foreground; 171, left, center, and right; 172; 173, foreground; 201, top left; 222, left: © Lori Weitzner.

Yurkevicz, Emily: 200, bottom left © 2014 Emily Yurkevicz.

Grateful acknowledgment is made for permission to quote from the following:

"Blue"
Words and Music by JONI MITCHELL
© 1971 (Renewed) CRAZY CROW MUSIC.
All Rights Administered by SONY/ATV MUSIC PUBLISHING, 8 Music Square West, Nashville, TN 37203. All Rights Reserved.

"Daffodowndilly" from *When We Were Very Young* by A.A. Milne. Text copyright © The Trustees of the Pooh Properties 1924. Published by Egmont UK Limited and used with permission.

"Daffodowndilly" by A.A. Milne, copyright 1924 by E.P. Dutton, renewed 1952 by A.A. Milne, from *When We Were Very Young* by A.A. Milne, illustrations by E.H. Shepard. Used by permission of Dutton Children's Books, an imprint of Penguin Young Readers Group, a division of Penguin Random House LLC.

Excerpt(s) from *Oh, the Places You'll Go!* by Dr. Seuss,™ and copyright © by Dr. Seuss Enterprises L.P. 1990. Used by permission of Random House Children's Books, a division of Penguin Random House LLC. All rights reserved. Any third party use of this material, outside of this publication, is prohibited. Interested parties must apply directly to Penguin Random House LLC for permission.

Ode to Color

HarperCollins books may be purchased for educational, business, or sales promotional use. For information please e-mail the Special Markets Department at SPsales@harpercollins.com.

First published in 2016 by
Harper Design
An Imprint of HarperCollins*Publishers*
195 Broadway
New York, NY 10007
Tel: (212) 207-7000
Fax: (855) 746-6023
www.hc.com
harperdesign@harpercollins.com

Distributed throughout the world by
HarperCollins*Publishers*
195 Broadway
New York, NY 10007

ISBN 978-0-06-239617-4
Library of Congress Control Number: 2014952861

Book design by: Niloo Tehranchi

Printed in China
First Printing, 2016